MATH PRACTICE WORKBOOK FOR 2ND GRADERS

WITH ANSWERS

 ADRISHYA CREATIONS

THIS WORKBOOK BELONGS TO

_____

_____

_____

Identifying Place Value

Identify and write the place value of the underlined numbers:

5̲14 =	Example:	5 hundreds	49̲ =	Example:	9 ones
75̲5 =	5 tens		8̲7 =		
62̲ =			9̲1 =		
9̲46 =			85̲7 =		
48̲ =			3̲7 =		
9̲ =			1̲6 =		
6̲64 =			5̲3 =		
42̲4 =			268̲ =		
20̲ =			7̲1 =		
8̲6 =			3̲2 =		
54̲1 =			7̲89 =		
3̲ =			6̲7 =		
95̲4 =			97̲ =		
7̲7 =			3̲62 =		
44̲ =			68̲9 =		

Identifying Place Value

Identify and write the place value of the underlined numbers:

$\underline{6}27 =$ _____	$2\underline{5} =$ _____
$8\underline{4}4 =$ _____	$\underline{4}2 =$ _____
$8\underline{7} =$ _____	$\underline{1}6 =$ _____
$\underline{7}48 =$ _____	$3\underline{6}3 =$ _____
$8\underline{4} =$ _____	$\underline{8}9 =$ _____
$\underline{8} =$ _____	$9\underline{0} =$ _____
$\underline{8}77 =$ _____	$\underline{7}4 =$ _____
$2\underline{7}1 =$ _____	$92\underline{5} =$ _____
$5\underline{3} =$ _____	$\underline{7}7 =$ _____
$\underline{4}4 =$ _____	$\underline{6}0 =$ _____
$1\underline{4}2 =$ _____	$\underline{1}65 =$ _____
$\underline{5} =$ _____	$\underline{9}6 =$ _____
$3\underline{1}4 =$ _____	$8\underline{8} =$ _____
$\underline{6}6 =$ _____	$\underline{8}37 =$ _____
$4\underline{9} =$ _____	$9\underline{7}8 =$ _____

Rounding Numbers

Round 2 digit numbers to the nearest 10:

Example:	$\underline{8}7 =$	90	Example:	$\underline{6}3 =$	60
1.)	$\underline{4}8 =$		14.)	$\underline{2}9 =$	
Example:	$\underline{1}5 =$	20	15.)	$\underline{3}1 =$	
2.)	$\underline{7}7 =$		16.)	$\underline{4}4 =$	
3.)	$\underline{7}9 =$		17.)	$\underline{7}8 =$	
4.)	$\underline{9}2 =$		18.)	$\underline{1}7 =$	
5.)	$\underline{8}7 =$		19.)	$\underline{8}2 =$	
6.)	$\underline{6}3 =$		20.)	$\underline{7}5 =$	
7.)	$\underline{4}2 =$		21.)	$\underline{7}4 =$	
8.)	$\underline{3}0 =$		22.)	$\underline{3}5 =$	
9.)	$\underline{5}9 =$		23.)	$\underline{1}4 =$	
10.)	$\underline{9}3 =$		24.)	$\underline{7}3 =$	
11.)	$\underline{9}6 =$		25.)	$\underline{7}4 =$	
12.)	$\underline{4}3 =$		26.)	$\underline{6}1 =$	
13.)	$\underline{3}7 =$		27.)	$\underline{9}9 =$	

Rounding Numbers

Round 3 digit numbers to the nearest 100:

Example:	$\underline{6}21$ =	600	Example:	$\underline{8}69$ =	900
Example:	$\underline{9}50$ =	1000	14.)	$\underline{1}86$ =	
1.)	$\underline{3}31$ =		15.)	$\underline{8}13$ =	
2.)	$\underline{6}52$ =		16.)	$\underline{8}00$ =	
3.)	$\underline{7}31$ =		17.)	$\underline{6}57$ =	
4.)	$\underline{7}67$ =		18.)	$\underline{4}48$ =	
5.)	$\underline{9}63$ =		19.)	$\underline{8}96$ =	
6.)	$\underline{4}08$ =		20.)	$\underline{2}45$ =	
7.)	$\underline{3}24$ =		21.)	$\underline{1}82$ =	
8.)	$\underline{5}63$ =		22.)	$\underline{8}34$ =	
9.)	$\underline{3}82$ =		23.)	$\underline{6}78$ =	
10.)	$\underline{2}79$ =		24.)	$\underline{6}49$ =	
11.)	$\underline{2}08$ =		25.)	$\underline{2}24$ =	
12.)	$\underline{2}81$ =		26.)	$\underline{9}64$ =	
13.)	$\underline{5}22$ =		27.)	$\underline{8}63$ =	

Rounding Numbers

Round 3 digit numbers to the nearest 10 or 100:

Example: 5<u>5</u>2 =	560	Example: <u>2</u>69 =	300
1.) 7<u>6</u>3 =		15.) 6<u>8</u>4 =	
2.) <u>9</u>03 =		16.) <u>4</u>22 =	
3.) <u>2</u>69 =		17.) <u>5</u>87 =	
4.) 7<u>8</u>3 =		18.) 1<u>5</u>6 =	
5.) 5<u>6</u>5 =		19.) 8<u>6</u>2 =	
6.) <u>5</u>11 =		20.) <u>6</u>78 =	
7.) 5<u>8</u>7 =		21.) 6<u>5</u>3 =	
8.) 7<u>1</u>3 =		22.) 8<u>5</u>6 =	
9.) <u>4</u>06 =		23.) <u>3</u>85 =	
10.) <u>6</u>28 =		24.) <u>7</u>87 =	
11.) 5<u>8</u>4 =		25.) 9<u>6</u>5 =	
12.) <u>7</u>58 =		26.) <u>6</u>45 =	
13.) 9<u>8</u>3 =		27.) 4<u>7</u>8 =	
14.) 1<u>3</u>4 =		28.) 9<u>1</u>0 =	

Adding 2 Digit Numbers

Add 2 digit numbers in columns (no carrying or regrouping):

Example:			
18 + 10 **28**	5.) 43 + 14	10.) 34 + 14	15.) 46 + 13
1.) 72 + 13	6.) 33 + 16	11.) 82 + 13	16.) 56 + 22
2.) 37 + 41	7.) 24 + 35	12.) 23 + 41	17.) 62 + 14
3.) 61 + 25	8.) 15 + 62	13.) 51 + 20	18.) 48 + 11
4.) 35 + 21	9.) 45 + 13	14.) 73 + 24	19.) 77 + 22

Adding 2 Digit Numbers

Add 2 digit numbers in columns (no carrying or regrouping):

1.) $\begin{array}{r} 18 \\ + 80 \\ \hline \end{array}$	6.) $\begin{array}{r} 70 \\ + 16 \\ \hline \end{array}$	11.) $\begin{array}{r} 17 \\ + 42 \\ \hline \end{array}$	16.) $\begin{array}{r} 14 \\ + 14 \\ \hline \end{array}$
2.) $\begin{array}{r} 16 \\ + 12 \\ \hline \end{array}$	7.) $\begin{array}{r} 30 \\ + 15 \\ \hline \end{array}$	12.) $\begin{array}{r} 62 \\ + 14 \\ \hline \end{array}$	17.) $\begin{array}{r} 86 \\ + 11 \\ \hline \end{array}$
3.) $\begin{array}{r} 57 \\ + 22 \\ \hline \end{array}$	8.) $\begin{array}{r} 19 \\ + 70 \\ \hline \end{array}$	13.) $\begin{array}{r} 33 \\ + 40 \\ \hline \end{array}$	18.) $\begin{array}{r} 13 \\ + 11 \\ \hline \end{array}$
4.) $\begin{array}{r} 41 \\ + 14 \\ \hline \end{array}$	9.) $\begin{array}{r} 61 \\ + 13 \\ \hline \end{array}$	14.) $\begin{array}{r} 31 \\ + 24 \\ \hline \end{array}$	19.) $\begin{array}{r} 54 \\ + 10 \\ \hline \end{array}$
5.) $\begin{array}{r} 64 \\ + 23 \\ \hline \end{array}$	10.) $\begin{array}{r} 83 \\ + 15 \\ \hline \end{array}$	15.) $\begin{array}{r} 71 \\ + 17 \\ \hline \end{array}$	20.) $\begin{array}{r} 44 \\ + 43 \\ \hline \end{array}$

Adding 2 Digit Numbers

Add 2 digit numbers in columns (no carrying or regrouping):

1.)
$$62 + 25$$

6.)
$$41 + 35$$

11.)
$$19 + 50$$

16.)
$$44 + 33$$

2.)
$$83 + 16$$

7.)
$$60 + 10$$

12.)
$$73 + 15$$

17.)
$$53 + 35$$

3.)
$$71 + 18$$

8.)
$$18 + 81$$

13.)
$$25 + 52$$

18.)
$$31 + 13$$

4.)
$$36 + 21$$

9.)
$$62 + 26$$

14.)
$$43 + 34$$

19.)
$$54 + 45$$

5.)
$$38 + 21$$

10.)
$$13 + 31$$

15.)
$$56 + 12$$

20.)
$$72 + 27$$

Adding 2 Digit Numbers

Add 2 digit numbers in columns (requires carrying or regrouping):

Example: 98 + 14 [112]	5.) 63 + 48	10.) 29 + 91	15.) 87 + 33
1.) 87 + 25	6.) 88 + 45	11.) 76 + 35	16.) 93 + 18
2.) 76 + 47	7.) 69 + 47	12.) 89 + 44	17.) 59 + 78
3.) 58 + 6	8.) 39 + 89	13.) 81 + 29	18.) 84 + 29
4.) 65 + 79	9.) 45 + 68	14.) 75 + 45	19.) 99 + 16

Adding 2 Digit Numbers

Add 2 digit numbers in columns (requires carrying or regrouping):

1.) $65 + 55$

2.) $79 + 63$

3.) $81 + 29$

4.) $94 + 27$

5.) $88 + 32$

6.) $94 + 26$

7.) $77 + 43$

8.) $99 + 76$

9.) $96 + 56$

10.) $29 + 82$

11.) $77 + 66$

12.) $78 + 45$

13.) $85 + 26$

14.) $87 + 24$

15.) $65 + 47$

16.) $96 + 15$

17.) $87 + 64$

18.) $89 + 43$

19.) $79 + 5$

20.) $67 + 59$

Adding 2 Digit Numbers

Add 2 digit numbers in columns (requires carrying or regrouping):

1.)
$$98$$
$$+\ 13$$

6.)
$$78$$
$$+\ 33$$

11.)
$$89$$
$$+\ 27$$

16.)
$$67$$
$$+\ 57$$

2.)
$$97$$
$$+\ 56$$

7.)
$$68$$
$$+\ 48$$

12.)
$$98$$
$$+\ 95$$

17.)
$$95$$
$$+\ 16$$

3.)
$$99$$
$$+\ 22$$

8.)
$$89$$
$$+\ 23$$

13.)
$$97$$
$$+\ 13$$

18.)
$$99$$
$$+\ 34$$

4.)
$$66$$
$$+\ 79$$

9.)
$$98$$
$$+\ 42$$

14.)
$$59$$
$$+\ 61$$

19.)
$$87$$
$$+\ 43$$

5.)
$$98$$
$$+\ 52$$

10.)
$$93$$
$$+\ 57$$

15.)
$$98$$
$$+\ 17$$

20.)
$$89$$
$$+\ 61$$

Adding 2 Digit Numbers

Add three 2 digit numbers in columns (requires carrying or regrouping):

Example: 58 56 + 27 **141**	4.) 93 58 + 14	8.) 59 22 + 25	12.) 44 25 + 15
1.) 24 66 + 40	5.) 38 47 + 21	9.) 64 34 + 53	13.) 39 67 + 36
2.) 33 64 + 17	6.) 56 61 + 51	10.) 65 49 + 21	14.) 61 41 + 82
3.) 61 85 + 24	7.) 75 53 + 54	11.) 40 56 + 54	15.) 86 73 + 66

Adding 2 Digit Numbers

Add three 2 digit numbers in columns (requires carrying or regrouping):

1.)
$$\begin{array}{r} 23 \\ 13 \\ + \ 54 \\ \hline \end{array}$$

5.)
$$\begin{array}{r} 54 \\ 68 \\ + \ 45 \\ \hline \end{array}$$

9.)
$$\begin{array}{r} 52 \\ 30 \\ + \ 88 \\ \hline \end{array}$$

13.)
$$\begin{array}{r} 72 \\ 21 \\ + \ 87 \\ \hline \end{array}$$

2.)
$$\begin{array}{r} 64 \\ 21 \\ + \ 97 \\ \hline \end{array}$$

6.)
$$\begin{array}{r} 89 \\ 16 \\ + \ 24 \\ \hline \end{array}$$

10.)
$$\begin{array}{r} 15 \\ 73 \\ + \ 14 \\ \hline \end{array}$$

14.)
$$\begin{array}{r} 62 \\ 31 \\ + \ 87 \\ \hline \end{array}$$

3.)
$$\begin{array}{r} 82 \\ 97 \\ + \ 62 \\ \hline \end{array}$$

7.)
$$\begin{array}{r} 20 \\ 56 \\ + \ 74 \\ \hline \end{array}$$

11.)
$$\begin{array}{r} 72 \\ 98 \\ + \ 82 \\ \hline \end{array}$$

15.)
$$\begin{array}{r} 37 \\ 44 \\ + \ 70 \\ \hline \end{array}$$

4.)
$$\begin{array}{r} 17 \\ 80 \\ + \ 14 \\ \hline \end{array}$$

8.)
$$\begin{array}{r} 51 \\ 13 \\ + \ 17 \\ \hline \end{array}$$

12.)
$$\begin{array}{r} 38 \\ 37 \\ + \ 70 \\ \hline \end{array}$$

16.)
$$\begin{array}{r} 49 \\ 26 \\ + \ 82 \\ \hline \end{array}$$

Adding 2 Digit Numbers

Add three 2 digit numbers in columns (requires carrying or regrouping):

1.)
```
   19
   17
+  45
```

5.)
```
   73
   65
+  78
```

9.)
```
   17
   54
+  20
```

13.)
```
   51
   21
+  69
```

2.)
```
   29
   57
+  28
```

6.)
```
   72
   29
+  11
```

10.)
```
   45
   91
+  15
```

14.)
```
   16
   35
+  19
```

3.)
```
   52
   72
+  64
```

7.)
```
   85
   62
+  24
```

11.)
```
   98
   24
+  32
```

15.)
```
   83
   48
+  71
```

4.)
```
   97
   95
+  67
```

8.)
```
   29
   17
+  30
```

12.)
```
   38
   23
+  27
```

16.)
```
   27
   87
+  81
```

Adding 2 Digit Numbers

Add four 2 digit numbers in columns (requires carrying or regrouping):

Example:

```
    17
    87
    41
  + 23
  ┌─────┐
  │ 168 │
  └─────┘
```

3.)
```
    19
    52
    92
  + 28
  ┌─────┐
  │     │
  └─────┘
```

6.)
```
    37
    25
    54
  + 44
  ┌─────┐
  │     │
  └─────┘
```

9.)
```
    87
    18
    43
  + 41
  ┌─────┐
  │     │
  └─────┘
```

1.)
```
    95
    78
    26
  + 51
  ┌─────┐
  │     │
  └─────┘
```

4.)
```
    35
    46
    33
  + 20
  ┌─────┐
  │     │
  └─────┘
```

7.)
```
    29
    46
    45
  + 60
  ┌─────┐
  │     │
  └─────┘
```

10.)
```
    87
    76
    19
  + 53
  ┌─────┐
  │     │
  └─────┘
```

2.)
```
    39
    41
    69
  + 60
  ┌─────┐
  │     │
  └─────┘
```

5.)
```
    41
    58
    29
  + 50
  ┌─────┐
  │     │
  └─────┘
```

8.)
```
    89
    55
    40
  + 33
  ┌─────┐
  │     │
  └─────┘
```

11.)
```
    67
    92
    75
  + 50
  ┌─────┐
  │     │
  └─────┘
```

Adding 2 Digit Numbers

Add four 2 digit numbers in columns (requires carrying or regrouping):

1.)   26
   25
   49
+ 69
	4.) 91
	   80
	   50
	+ 22
		7.) 83
		   28
		   45
		+ 15
			10.) 47
			   27
			   21
			+ 44

2.)   25
   39
   87
+ 95
	5.) 62
	   73
	   57
	+ 71
		8.) 97
		   74
		   95
		+ 13
			11.) 52
			   94
			   92
			+ 60

3.)   65
   40
   22
+ 30
	6.) 24
	   39
	   47
	+ 64
		9.) 61
		   13
		   76
		+ 74
			12.) 65
			   24
			   66
			+ 44

Adding 2 Digit Numbers

Add four 2 digit numbers in columns (requires carrying or regrouping):

1.)
```
    27
    47
    75
  + 22
```

4.)
```
    54
    95
    62
  + 94
```

7.)
```
    67
    92
    97
  + 63
```

10.)
```
    68
    50
    42
  + 60
```

2.)
```
    91
    88
    63
  + 43
```

5.)
```
    82
    12
    39
  + 41
```

8.)
```
    95
    52
    24
  + 84
```

11.)
```
    93
    72
    36
  + 70
```

3.)
```
    26
    60
    21
  + 55
```

6.)
```
    29
    69
    12
  + 34
```

9.)
```
    41
    78
    31
  + 58
```

12.)
```
    63
    42
    50
  + 35
```

Adding 3 Digit Numbers

Add 3 digit numbers in columns (no carrying or regrouping):

Example:	5.)	10.)	15.)
873 $+\ 111$	178 $+\ 821$	392 $+\ 303$	114 $+\ 142$
$\boxed{984}$	$\Box$	$\Box$	$\Box$

1.)	6.)	11.)	16.)
657 $+\ 221$	307 $+\ 121$	562 $+\ 107$	233 $+\ 654$
$\Box$	$\Box$	$\Box$	$\Box$

2.)	7.)	12.)	17.)
788 $+\ 201$	429 $+\ 260$	296 $+\ 402$	474 $+\ 222$
$\Box$	$\Box$	$\Box$	$\Box$

3.)	8.)	13.)	18.)
847 $+\ 122$	602 $+\ 172$	124 $+\ 351$	311 $+\ 166$
$\Box$	$\Box$	$\Box$	$\Box$

4.)	9.)	14.)	19.)
800 $+\ 159$	432 $+\ 226$	168 $+\ 711$	834 $+\ 144$
$\Box$	$\Box$	$\Box$	$\Box$

Adding 3 Digit Numbers

Add 3 digit numbers in columns (no carrying or regrouping):

1.) $441 + 417$	6.) $291 + 406$	11.) $337 + 442$	16.) $236 + 342$
2.) $253 + 522$	7.) $870 + 107$	12.) $833 + 143$	17.) $447 + 521$
3.) $281 + 608$	8.) $219 + 420$	13.) $665 + 134$	18.) $215 + 381$
4.) $443 + 546$	9.) $254 + 401$	14.) $601 + 295$	19.) $623 + 112$
5.) $168 + 331$	10.) $862 + 135$	15.) $201 + 613$	20.) $514 + 203$

Adding 3 Digit Numbers

Add 3 digit numbers in columns (no carrying or regrouping):

1.) 425
   + 222

6.) 742
   + 211

11.) 246
   + 253

16.) 603
   + 205

2.) 358
   + 131

7.) 792
   + 106

12.) 645
   + 334

17.) 452
   + 413

3.) 624
   + 241

8.) 408
   + 311

13.) 641
   + 118

18.) 773
   + 202

4.) 833
   + 114

9.) 801
   + 128

14.) 751
   + 121

19.) 246
   + 401

5.) 314
   + 275

10.) 205
   + 604

15.) 304
   + 142

20.) 740
   + 108

Adding 3 Digit Numbers

Add 3 digit numbers in columns (requires carrying or regrouping):

Example:			
788 + 569 **1357**	5.) 894 + 426	10.) 681 + 589	15.) 977 + 149
1.) 862 + 656	6.) 916 + 698	11.) 894 + 525	16.) 761 + 356
2.) 762 + 471	7.) 897 + 737	12.) 213 + 883	17.) 753 + 578
3.) 856 + 284	8.) 949 + 272	13.) 863 + 278	18.) 887 + 617
4.) 983 + 377	9.) 981 + 579	14.) 972 + 387	19.) 899 + 343

Adding 3 Digit Numbers

Add 3 digit numbers in columns (requires carrying or regrouping):

1.) $\begin{array}{r} 777 \\ +\ 523 \\ \hline \end{array}$	6.) $\begin{array}{r} 867 \\ +\ 288 \\ \hline \end{array}$	11.) $\begin{array}{r} 922 \\ +\ 498 \\ \hline \end{array}$	16.) $\begin{array}{r} 899 \\ +\ 314 \\ \hline \end{array}$
2.) $\begin{array}{r} 899 \\ +\ 241 \\ \hline \end{array}$	7.) $\begin{array}{r} 869 \\ +\ 267 \\ \hline \end{array}$	12.) $\begin{array}{r} 899 \\ +\ 732 \\ \hline \end{array}$	17.) $\begin{array}{r} 799 \\ +\ 312 \\ \hline \end{array}$
3.) $\begin{array}{r} 888 \\ +\ 112 \\ \hline \end{array}$	8.) $\begin{array}{r} 964 \\ +\ 135 \\ \hline \end{array}$	13.) $\begin{array}{r} 844 \\ +\ 478 \\ \hline \end{array}$	18.) $\begin{array}{r} 978 \\ +\ 154 \\ \hline \end{array}$
4.) $\begin{array}{r} 899 \\ +\ 313 \\ \hline \end{array}$	9.) $\begin{array}{r} 927 \\ +\ 814 \\ \hline \end{array}$	14.) $\begin{array}{r} 699 \\ +\ 199 \\ \hline \end{array}$	19.) $\begin{array}{r} 937 \\ +\ 298 \\ \hline \end{array}$
5.) $\begin{array}{r} 975 \\ +\ 339 \\ \hline \end{array}$	10.) $\begin{array}{r} 899 \\ +\ 344 \\ \hline \end{array}$	15.) $\begin{array}{r} 969 \\ +\ 144 \\ \hline \end{array}$	20.) $\begin{array}{r} 968 \\ +\ 327 \\ \hline \end{array}$

Adding 3 Digit Numbers

Add 3 digit numbers in columns (requires carrying or regrouping):

1.) $\begin{array}{r}864\\+278\\\hline\end{array}$	6.) $\begin{array}{r}866\\+367\\\hline\end{array}$	11.) $\begin{array}{r}976\\+154\\\hline\end{array}$	16.) $\begin{array}{r}862\\+559\\\hline\end{array}$
2.) $\begin{array}{r}979\\+927\\\hline\end{array}$	7.) $\begin{array}{r}862\\+449\\\hline\end{array}$	12.) $\begin{array}{r}870\\+549\\\hline\end{array}$	17.) $\begin{array}{r}675\\+768\\\hline\end{array}$
3.) $\begin{array}{r}997\\+114\\\hline\end{array}$	8.) $\begin{array}{r}792\\+358\\\hline\end{array}$	13.) $\begin{array}{r}569\\+554\\\hline\end{array}$	18.) $\begin{array}{r}799\\+721\\\hline\end{array}$
4.) $\begin{array}{r}891\\+912\\\hline\end{array}$	9.) $\begin{array}{r}716\\+696\\\hline\end{array}$	14.) $\begin{array}{r}987\\+453\\\hline\end{array}$	19.) $\begin{array}{r}939\\+193\\\hline\end{array}$
5.) $\begin{array}{r}996\\+324\\\hline\end{array}$	10.) $\begin{array}{r}942\\+669\\\hline\end{array}$	15.) $\begin{array}{r}796\\+815\\\hline\end{array}$	20.) $\begin{array}{r}712\\+390\\\hline\end{array}$

Adding 3 Digit Numbers

Add three 3 digit numbers in columns (requires carrying or regrouping):

Example:			
756 111 + 461 **1320**	4.) 765 685 + 362	8.) 838 254 + 980	12.) 481 185 + 282
1.) 741 622 + 420	5.) 675 419 + 951	9.) 681 132 + 860	13.) 879 646 + 960
2.) 927 917 + 660	6.) 959 484 + 117	10.) 829 291 + 377	14.) 873 597 + 466
3.) 694 371 + 517	7.) 970 282 + 371	11.) 894 799 + 650	15.) 478 308 + 261

Adding 3 Digit Numbers

Add three 3 digit numbers in columns (requires carrying or regrouping):

1.)
$$\begin{array}{r} 811 \\ 817 \\ +\ 691 \\ \hline \end{array}$$

5.)
$$\begin{array}{r} 835 \\ 496 \\ +\ 639 \\ \hline \end{array}$$

9.)
$$\begin{array}{r} 702 \\ 403 \\ +\ 322 \\ \hline \end{array}$$

13.)
$$\begin{array}{r} 820 \\ 304 \\ +\ 273 \\ \hline \end{array}$$

2.)
$$\begin{array}{r} 547 \\ 358 \\ +\ 366 \\ \hline \end{array}$$

6.)
$$\begin{array}{r} 881 \\ 495 \\ +\ 320 \\ \hline \end{array}$$

10.)
$$\begin{array}{r} 559 \\ 351 \\ +\ 139 \\ \hline \end{array}$$

14.)
$$\begin{array}{r} 530 \\ 307 \\ +\ 175 \\ \hline \end{array}$$

3.)
$$\begin{array}{r} 566 \\ 358 \\ +\ 335 \\ \hline \end{array}$$

7.)
$$\begin{array}{r} 478 \\ 412 \\ +\ 123 \\ \hline \end{array}$$

11.)
$$\begin{array}{r} 665 \\ 479 \\ +\ 115 \\ \hline \end{array}$$

15.)
$$\begin{array}{r} 420 \\ 277 \\ +\ 139 \\ \hline \end{array}$$

4.)
$$\begin{array}{r} 368 \\ 415 \\ +\ 710 \\ \hline \end{array}$$

8.)
$$\begin{array}{r} 767 \\ 713 \\ +\ 278 \\ \hline \end{array}$$

12.)
$$\begin{array}{r} 665 \\ 586 \\ +\ 690 \\ \hline \end{array}$$

16.)
$$\begin{array}{r} 943 \\ 604 \\ +\ 110 \\ \hline \end{array}$$

Adding 3 Digit Numbers

Add three 3 digit numbers in columns (requires carrying or regrouping):

1.)
$$571$$
$$502$$
$$+\ 296$$

5.)
$$305$$
$$291$$
$$+\ 142$$

9.)
$$540$$
$$872$$
$$+\ 580$$

13.)
$$961$$
$$725$$
$$+\ 691$$

2.)
$$763$$
$$662$$
$$+\ 421$$

6.)
$$944$$
$$558$$
$$+\ 430$$

10.)
$$574$$
$$420$$
$$+\ 415$$

14.)
$$976$$
$$560$$
$$+\ 141$$

3.)
$$810$$
$$453$$
$$+\ 241$$

7.)
$$847$$
$$435$$
$$+\ 432$$

11.)
$$751$$
$$563$$
$$+\ 180$$

15.)
$$935$$
$$598$$
$$+\ 446$$

4.)
$$572$$
$$351$$
$$+\ 157$$

8.)
$$860$$
$$218$$
$$+\ 176$$

12.)
$$848$$
$$380$$
$$+\ 430$$

16.)
$$749$$
$$717$$
$$+\ 356$$

Subtracting 2 Digit Numbers

Subtract 2 digit numbers in columns (no borrowing or regrouping):

Example:			
26 - 24 **2**	5.) 36 - 14	10.) 24 - 11	15.) 17 - 12
1.) 14 - 10	6.) 68 - 23	11.) 48 - 24	16.) 95 - 13
2.) 87 - 10	7.) 67 - 43	12.) 63 - 21	17.) 87 - 42
3.) 12 - 11	8.) 87 - 15	13.) 72 - 52	18.) 64 - 30
4.) 36 - 13	9.) 76 - 72	14.) 55 - 25	19.) 86 - 36

Subtracting 2 Digit Numbers

Subtract 2 digit numbers in columns (no borrowing or regrouping):

1.) 98 − 64	6.) 75 − 14	11.) 62 − 11	16.) 19 − 10
2.) 82 − 21	7.) 95 − 53	12.) 69 − 17	17.) 54 − 41
3.) 67 − 56	8.) 89 − 26	13.) 66 − 21	18.) 28 − 22
4.) 22 − 11	9.) 78 − 16	14.) 53 − 20	19.) 59 − 55
5.) 43 − 13	10.) 67 − 24	15.) 53 − 22	20.) 68 − 25

Subtracting 2 Digit Numbers

Subtract 2 digit numbers in columns (no borrowing or regrouping):

1.) $\begin{array}{r} 45 \\ -\ 42 \\ \hline \end{array}$	6.) $\begin{array}{r} 96 \\ -\ 13 \\ \hline \end{array}$	11.) $\begin{array}{r} 35 \\ -\ 14 \\ \hline \end{array}$	16.) $\begin{array}{r} 72 \\ -\ 51 \\ \hline \end{array}$
2.) $\begin{array}{r} 85 \\ -\ 32 \\ \hline \end{array}$	7.) $\begin{array}{r} 48 \\ -\ 35 \\ \hline \end{array}$	12.) $\begin{array}{r} 45 \\ -\ 14 \\ \hline \end{array}$	17.) $\begin{array}{r} 59 \\ -\ 46 \\ \hline \end{array}$
3.) $\begin{array}{r} 34 \\ -\ 30 \\ \hline \end{array}$	8.) $\begin{array}{r} 90 \\ -\ 50 \\ \hline \end{array}$	13.) $\begin{array}{r} 28 \\ -\ 19 \\ \hline \end{array}$	18.) $\begin{array}{r} 99 \\ -\ 22 \\ \hline \end{array}$
4.) $\begin{array}{r} 87 \\ -\ 14 \\ \hline \end{array}$	9.) $\begin{array}{r} 26 \\ -\ 16 \\ \hline \end{array}$	14.) $\begin{array}{r} 69 \\ -\ 28 \\ \hline \end{array}$	19.) $\begin{array}{r} 79 \\ -\ 55 \\ \hline \end{array}$
5.) $\begin{array}{r} 57 \\ -\ 13 \\ \hline \end{array}$	10.) $\begin{array}{r} 66 \\ -\ 34 \\ \hline \end{array}$	15.) $\begin{array}{r} 83 \\ -\ 22 \\ \hline \end{array}$	20.) $\begin{array}{r} 95 \\ -\ 35 \\ \hline \end{array}$

Subtracting 2 Digit Numbers

Subtract 2 digit numbers in columns (requires borrowing or regrouping):

Example:			

94
- 17
77
	5.) 86
	   - 38
		10.) 64
		   - 18
			15.) 91
			   - 89

1.)   95
   - 67
	6.) 74
	   - 19
		11.) 75
		   - 56
			16.) 76
			   - 67

2.)   81
   - 25
	7.) 72
	   - 57
		12.) 48
		   - 39
			17.) 52
			   - 33

3.)   62
   - 48
	8.) 94
	   - 65
		13.) 71
		   - 53
			18.) 41
			   - 23

4.)   95
   - 18
	9.) 86
	   - 57
		14.) 51
		   - 42
			19.) 72
			   - 63

Subtracting 2 Digit Numbers

Subtract 2 digit numbers in columns (requires borrowing or regrouping):

1.) 71 − 42	6.) 92 − 43	11.) 63 − 54	16.) 85 − 66
2.) 52 − 28	7.) 91 − 76	12.) 91 − 83	17.) 62 − 45
3.) 61 − 52	8.) 51 − 32	13.) 70 − 21	18.) 81 − 73
4.) 85 − 39	9.) 97 − 89	14.) 93 − 34	19.) 93 − 67
5.) 91 − 72	10.) 32 − 19	15.) 92 − 88	20.) 85 − 68

Subtracting 2 Digit Numbers

Subtract 2 digit numbers in columns (requires borrowing or regrouping):

1.) 87 − 79	6.) 61 − 42	11.) 71 − 53	16.) 91 − 56
2.) 21 − 12	7.) 71 − 54	12.) 62 − 47	17.) 94 − 36
3.) 93 − 65	8.) 81 − 55	13.) 92 − 58	18.) 93 − 85
4.) 23 − 14	9.) 71 − 43	14.) 94 − 87	19.) 81 − 44
5.) 51 − 12	10.) 81 − 62	15.) 36 − 18	20.) 87 − 29

Subtracting 3 Digit Numbers

Subtract 3 digit numbers in columns (no borrowing or regrouping):

Example:			
967 - 106 **861**	5.) 496 - 133	10.) 897 - 850	15.) 549 - 408
1.) 306 - 202	6.) 159 - 141	11.) 645 - 614	16.) 380 - 240
2.) 343 - 123	7.) 868 - 416	12.) 905 - 104	17.) 376 - 310
3.) 954 - 913	8.) 620 - 310	13.) 235 - 122	18.) 703 - 210
4.) 227 - 125	9.) 934 - 430	14.) 512 - 111	19.) 325 - 301

Subtracting 3 Digit Numbers

Subtract 3 digit numbers in columns (no borrowing or regrouping):

1.) 903 − 303	6.) 942 − 341	11.) 436 − 215	16.) 884 − 754
2.) 862 − 241	7.) 249 − 148	12.) 335 − 111	17.) 722 − 521
3.) 289 − 261	8.) 287 − 161	13.) 968 − 560	18.) 640 − 530
4.) 692 − 280	9.) 585 − 183	14.) 686 − 422	19.) 814 − 701
5.) 508 − 102	10.) 607 − 503	15.) 788 − 745	20.) 612 − 510

Subtracting 3 Digit Numbers

Subtract 3 digit numbers in columns (no borrowing or regrouping):

1.) 126 − 106	6.) 415 − 212	11.) 435 − 313	16.) 467 − 263
2.) 981 − 860	7.) 366 − 244	12.) 433 − 111	17.) 885 − 534
3.) 166 − 145	8.) 284 − 252	13.) 459 − 214	18.) 387 − 210
4.) 802 − 601	9.) 697 − 341	14.) 658 − 324	19.) 721 − 410
5.) 527 − 112	10.) 154 − 143	15.) 676 − 423	20.) 978 − 538

Subtracting 3 Digit Numbers

Subtract 3 digit numbers in columns (requires borrowing or regrouping):

Example:			
993 - 886 **107**	5.) 965 - 859	10.) 720 - 418	15.) 298 - 186
1.) 893 - 678	6.) 786 - 419	11.) 693 - 274	16.) 480 - 264
2.) 540 - 450	7.) 924 - 806	12.) 491 - 384	17.) 961 - 403
3.) 792 - 387	8.) 996 - 878	13.) 482 - 327	18.) 951 - 642
4.) 781 - 164	9.) 738 - 125	14.) 481 - 352	19.) 812 - 306

Subtracting 3 Digit Numbers

Subtract 3 digit numbers in columns (requires borrowing or regrouping):

1.) $\begin{array}{r}910 \\ -\ 821 \\ \hline\end{array}$	6.) $\begin{array}{r}580 \\ -\ 433 \\ \hline\end{array}$	11.) $\begin{array}{r}814 \\ -\ 407 \\ \hline\end{array}$	16.) $\begin{array}{r}981 \\ -\ 862 \\ \hline\end{array}$
2.) $\begin{array}{r}782 \\ -\ 433 \\ \hline\end{array}$	7.) $\begin{array}{r}961 \\ -\ 482 \\ \hline\end{array}$	12.) $\begin{array}{r}995 \\ -\ 678 \\ \hline\end{array}$	17.) $\begin{array}{r}943 \\ -\ 847 \\ \hline\end{array}$
3.) $\begin{array}{r}600 \\ -\ 252 \\ \hline\end{array}$	8.) $\begin{array}{r}741 \\ -\ 512 \\ \hline\end{array}$	13.) $\begin{array}{r}673 \\ -\ 234 \\ \hline\end{array}$	18.) $\begin{array}{r}870 \\ -\ 421 \\ \hline\end{array}$
4.) $\begin{array}{r}790 \\ -\ 286 \\ \hline\end{array}$	9.) $\begin{array}{r}980 \\ -\ 842 \\ \hline\end{array}$	14.) $\begin{array}{r}995 \\ -\ 889 \\ \hline\end{array}$	19.) $\begin{array}{r}973 \\ -\ 507 \\ \hline\end{array}$
5.) $\begin{array}{r}740 \\ -\ 102 \\ \hline\end{array}$	10.) $\begin{array}{r}685 \\ -\ 449 \\ \hline\end{array}$	15.) $\begin{array}{r}231 \\ -\ 125 \\ \hline\end{array}$	20.) $\begin{array}{r}881 \\ -\ 406 \\ \hline\end{array}$

Subtracting 3 Digit Numbers

Subtract 3 digit numbers in columns (requires borrowing or regrouping):

1.) $\begin{array}{r} 442 \\ -\ 338 \\ \hline \end{array}$	6.) $\begin{array}{r} 972 \\ -\ 165 \\ \hline \end{array}$	11.) $\begin{array}{r} 310 \\ -\ 132 \\ \hline \end{array}$	16.) $\begin{array}{r} 986 \\ -\ 678 \\ \hline \end{array}$
2.) $\begin{array}{r} 851 \\ -\ 615 \\ \hline \end{array}$	7.) $\begin{array}{r} 380 \\ -\ 188 \\ \hline \end{array}$	12.) $\begin{array}{r} 634 \\ -\ 315 \\ \hline \end{array}$	17.) $\begin{array}{r} 543 \\ -\ 369 \\ \hline \end{array}$
3.) $\begin{array}{r} 863 \\ -\ 124 \\ \hline \end{array}$	8.) $\begin{array}{r} 892 \\ -\ 784 \\ \hline \end{array}$	13.) $\begin{array}{r} 681 \\ -\ 273 \\ \hline \end{array}$	18.) $\begin{array}{r} 480 \\ -\ 272 \\ \hline \end{array}$
4.) $\begin{array}{r} 793 \\ -\ 277 \\ \hline \end{array}$	9.) $\begin{array}{r} 692 \\ -\ 538 \\ \hline \end{array}$	14.) $\begin{array}{r} 692 \\ -\ 385 \\ \hline \end{array}$	19.) $\begin{array}{r} 387 \\ -\ 189 \\ \hline \end{array}$
5.) $\begin{array}{r} 832 \\ -\ 315 \\ \hline \end{array}$	10.) $\begin{array}{r} 981 \\ -\ 348 \\ \hline \end{array}$	15.) $\begin{array}{r} 990 \\ -\ 884 \\ \hline \end{array}$	20.) $\begin{array}{r} 693 \\ -\ 265 \\ \hline \end{array}$

Multiplication Tables

Fill the box with the correct answer:

1.)	$1 \times 1 =$		11.)	$2 \times 1 =$	
2.)	$1 \times 2 =$		12.)	$2 \times 2 =$	
3.)	$1 \times 3 =$		13.)	$2 \times 3 =$	
4.)	$1 \times 4 =$		14.)	$2 \times 4 =$	
5.)	$1 \times 5 =$		15.)	$2 \times 5 =$	
6.)	$1 \times 6 =$		16.)	$2 \times 6 =$	
7.)	$1 \times 7 =$		17.)	$2 \times 7 =$	
8.)	$1 \times 8 =$		18.)	$2 \times 8 =$	
9.)	$1 \times 9 =$		19.)	$2 \times 9 =$	
10.)	$1 \times 10 =$		20.	$2 \times 10 =$	

Multiplication Tables

Fill the box with the correct answer:

1.)	$3 \times 1 =$		11.)	$4 \times 1 =$
2.)	$3 \times 2 =$		12.)	$4 \times 2 =$
3.)	$3 \times 3 =$		13.)	$4 \times 3 =$
4.)	$3 \times 4 =$		14.)	$4 \times 4 =$
5.)	$3 \times 5 =$		15.)	$4 \times 5 =$
6.)	$3 \times 6 =$		16.)	$4 \times 6 =$
7.)	$3 \times 7 =$		17.)	$4 \times 7 =$
8.)	$3 \times 8 =$		18.)	$4 \times 8 =$
9.)	$3 \times 9 =$		19.)	$4 \times 9 =$
10.)	$3 \times 10 =$		20.	$4 \times 10 =$

Multiplication Tables

Fill the box with the correct answer:

1.)	$5 \times 1 =$		11.)	$6 \times 1 =$
2.)	$5 \times 2 =$		12.)	$6 \times 2 =$
3.)	$5 \times 3 =$		13.)	$6 \times 3 =$
4.)	$5 \times 4 =$		14.)	$6 \times 4 =$
5.)	$5 \times 5 =$		15.)	$6 \times 5 =$
6.)	$5 \times 6 =$		16.)	$6 \times 6 =$
7.)	$5 \times 7 =$		17.)	$6 \times 7 =$
8.)	$5 \times 8 =$		18.)	$6 \times 8 =$
9.)	$5 \times 9 =$		19.)	$6 \times 9 =$
10.)	$5 \times 10 =$		20.	$6 \times 10 =$

Multiplication Tables

Fill the box with the correct answer:

1.) $7 \times 1 =$	11.) $8 \times 1 =$
2.) $7 \times 2 =$	12.) $8 \times 2 =$
3.) $7 \times 3 =$	13.) $8 \times 3 =$
4.) $7 \times 4 =$	14.) $8 \times 4 =$
5.) $7 \times 5 =$	15.) $8 \times 5 =$
6.) $7 \times 6 =$	16.) $8 \times 6 =$
7.) $7 \times 7 =$	17.) $8 \times 7 =$
8.) $7 \times 8 =$	18.) $8 \times 8 =$
9.) $7 \times 9 =$	19.) $8 \times 9 =$
10.) $7 \times 10 =$	20. $8 \times 10 =$

Multiplication Tables

Fill the box with the correct answer:

1.)	$9 \times 1 =$	11.)	$10 \times 1 =$
2.)	$9 \times 2 =$	12.)	$10 \times 2 =$
3.)	$9 \times 3 =$	13.)	$10 \times 3 =$
4.)	$9 \times 4 =$	14.)	$10 \times 4 =$
5.)	$9 \times 5 =$	15.)	$10 \times 5 =$
6.)	$9 \times 6 =$	16.)	$10 \times 6 =$
7.)	$9 \times 7 =$	17.)	$10 \times 7 =$
8.)	$9 \times 8 =$	18.)	$10 \times 8 =$
9.)	$9 \times 9 =$	19.)	$10 \times 9 =$
10.	$9 \times 10 =$	20.)	$10 \times 10 =$

Basic Fractions: Identify Halves

Color half of each geometric shapes which are divided into two equal parts:

1.)	5.)	**Example:**
2.)	6.)	9.)
3.)	7.)	10.)
4.)	8.)	11.)

Basic Fractions: Identify Thirds

Circle each geometric shapes which are divided into thirds (three equal parts):

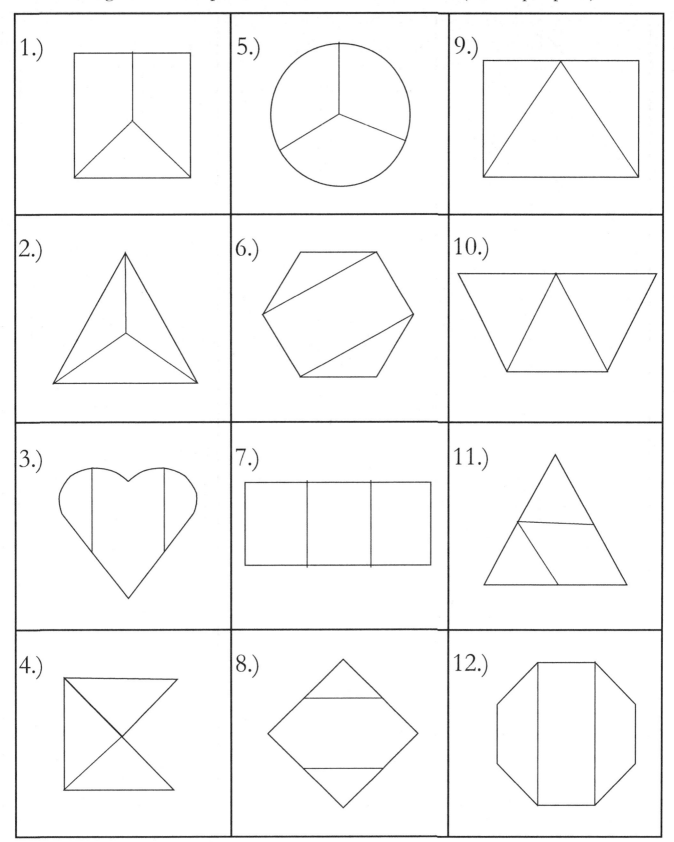

Basic Fractions: Identify Quarters

Circle each geometric shapes which are divided into quarters (four equal parts):

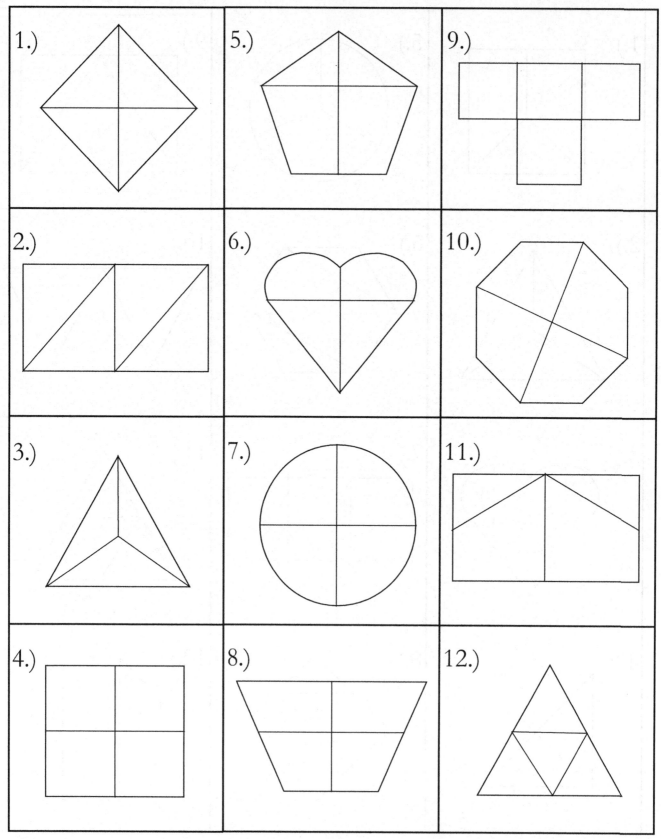

Numerators & Denominators

Identify Numerators (top no. in the fraction) & Denominators (bottom no.):

Fraction		Numerator	Denominator
Example: $\dfrac{1}{2}$		1	2
1.) $\dfrac{1}{3}$			
2.) $\dfrac{1}{4}$			
3.) $\dfrac{3}{5}$			
4.) $\dfrac{3}{6}$			
5.) $\dfrac{4}{8}$			
6.) $\dfrac{2}{6}$			

Numerators & Denominators

Identify Numerators (top no. in the fraction) & Denominators (bottom no.):

Fraction		Numerator	Denominator
1.) $\dfrac{2}{3}$			
2.) $\dfrac{2}{4}$			
3.) $\dfrac{2}{5}$			
4.) $\dfrac{1}{6}$			
5.) $\dfrac{4}{6}$			
6.) $\dfrac{3}{8}$			
7.) $\dfrac{2}{8}$			

Write Fractions

Write fractions from Numerators and Denominators:

Fraction		Numerator	Denominator
Example: $\dfrac{2}{6}$		2	6
1.)		4	8
2.)		3	6
3.)		3	5
4.)		1	4
5.)		1	3
6.)		1	2

Write Fractions

Write fractions from Numerators and Denominators:

Fraction		Numerator	Denominator
1.)		2	8
2.)		3	8
3.)		4	6
4.)		1	6
5.)		2	5
6.)		2	4
7.)		2	3

Reading Fractions

Draw lines to match fractions to the words:

$\dfrac{1}{2}$	One Third
$\dfrac{1}{3}$	Two Thirds
$\dfrac{1}{4}$	One Half
$\dfrac{1}{6}$	Three Quarters
$\dfrac{2}{3}$	One Quarter
$\dfrac{3}{4}$	One Sixth

Reading Fractions

Draw lines to match fractions to the words:

$\dfrac{9}{10}$	Two Thirds
$\dfrac{5}{6}$	One Quarter
$\dfrac{2}{4}$	Nine Tenths
$\dfrac{1}{8}$	Two Quarters
$\dfrac{1}{4}$	Five Sixths
$\dfrac{2}{3}$	One Eighth

Reading Fractions

Draw lines to match fractions to the words:

$\frac{3}{4}$	One Fifth
$\frac{1}{5}$	Seven Eights
$\frac{2}{7}$	Three Quarters
$\frac{7}{8}$	Three Sixths
$\frac{3}{6}$	Two Eights
$\frac{2}{8}$	Two Sevenths

Identify Fractions

Match fractions to pictures, circle the correct answer:

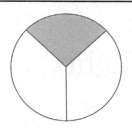 **Example:**	$\dfrac{1}{6}$	$\dfrac{3}{7}$	$\dfrac{1}{2}$	$\dfrac{1}{4}$
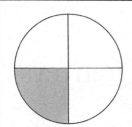	$\dfrac{1}{4}$	$\dfrac{1}{3}$	$\dfrac{1}{7}$	$\dfrac{1}{2}$
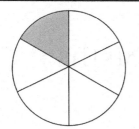	$\dfrac{4}{4}$	$\dfrac{3}{4}$	$\dfrac{2}{4}$	$\dfrac{1}{4}$
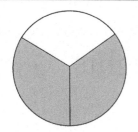	$\dfrac{2}{3}$	$\dfrac{1}{6}$	$\dfrac{2}{6}$	$\dfrac{1}{3}$
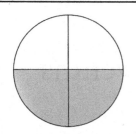	$\dfrac{1}{3}$	$\dfrac{2}{3}$	$\dfrac{1}{6}$	$\dfrac{3}{3}$
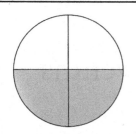	$\dfrac{1}{4}$	$\dfrac{1}{3}$	$\dfrac{2}{4}$	$\dfrac{2}{3}$

Identify Fractions

Match fractions to the shaded circles and circle the correct answer:

◉ ○	**Example:** $\dfrac{1}{6}$ $\dfrac{3}{7}$ $\left(\dfrac{1}{2}\right)$ $\dfrac{1}{4}$
◉ ○ ○	$\dfrac{1}{4}$ $\dfrac{1}{3}$ $\dfrac{1}{7}$ $\dfrac{1}{2}$
◉ ◉ ○ ◉ ○	$\dfrac{4}{4}$ $\dfrac{3}{5}$ $\dfrac{2}{4}$ $\dfrac{1}{4}$
◉ ◉ ○ ◉ ○ ○	$\dfrac{2}{3}$ $\dfrac{1}{6}$ $\dfrac{3}{6}$ $\dfrac{1}{3}$
◉ ◉ ○ ○ ◉ ◉ ○ ○	$\dfrac{1}{3}$ $\dfrac{4}{8}$ $\dfrac{1}{6}$ $\dfrac{3}{8}$
◉ ◉ ○ ○ ○ ○	$\dfrac{1}{4}$ $\dfrac{1}{3}$ $\dfrac{2}{4}$ $\dfrac{2}{6}$

Identify Fractions

Match fractions to the shaded circles and circle the correct answer:

	Example: $\dfrac{1}{6}$	$\dfrac{3}{4}$	$\dfrac{1}{2}$	$\left(\dfrac{2}{4}\right)$
	$\dfrac{1}{4}$	$\dfrac{2}{5}$	$\dfrac{5}{4}$	$\dfrac{1}{2}$
	$\dfrac{4}{4}$	$\dfrac{1}{5}$	$\dfrac{2}{5}$	$\dfrac{1}{6}$
	$\dfrac{2}{3}$	$\dfrac{5}{6}$	$\dfrac{4}{6}$	$\dfrac{1}{3}$
	$\dfrac{1}{3}$	$\dfrac{4}{8}$	$\dfrac{1}{6}$	$\dfrac{3}{8}$
	$\dfrac{1}{4}$	$\dfrac{1}{8}$	$\dfrac{2}{8}$	$\dfrac{2}{9}$

Identify Fractions

Color the shapes according to the shown fractions:

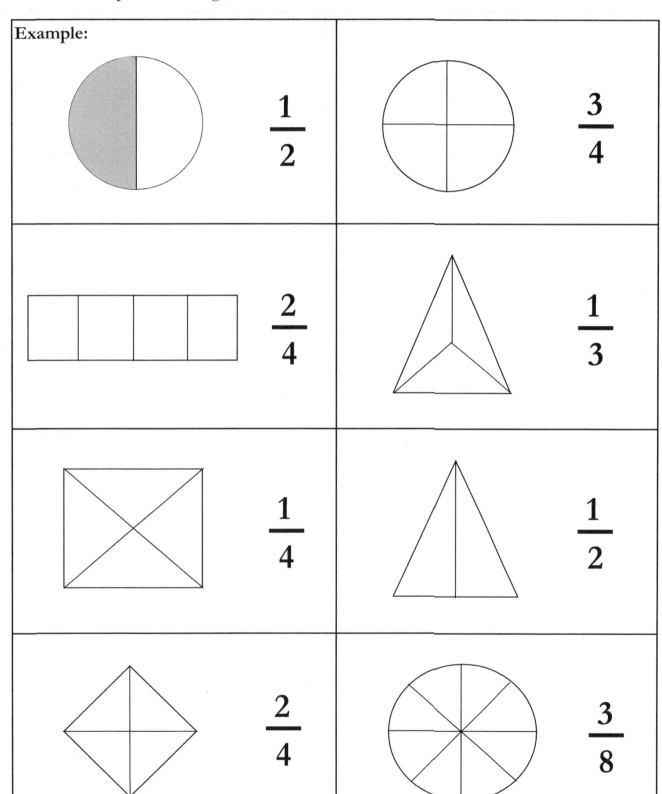

Example:

$\dfrac{1}{2}$

$\dfrac{3}{4}$

$\dfrac{2}{4}$

$\dfrac{1}{3}$

$\dfrac{1}{4}$

$\dfrac{1}{2}$

$\dfrac{2}{4}$

$\dfrac{3}{8}$

Identify Fractions

Write the fractions according to the colored shapes:

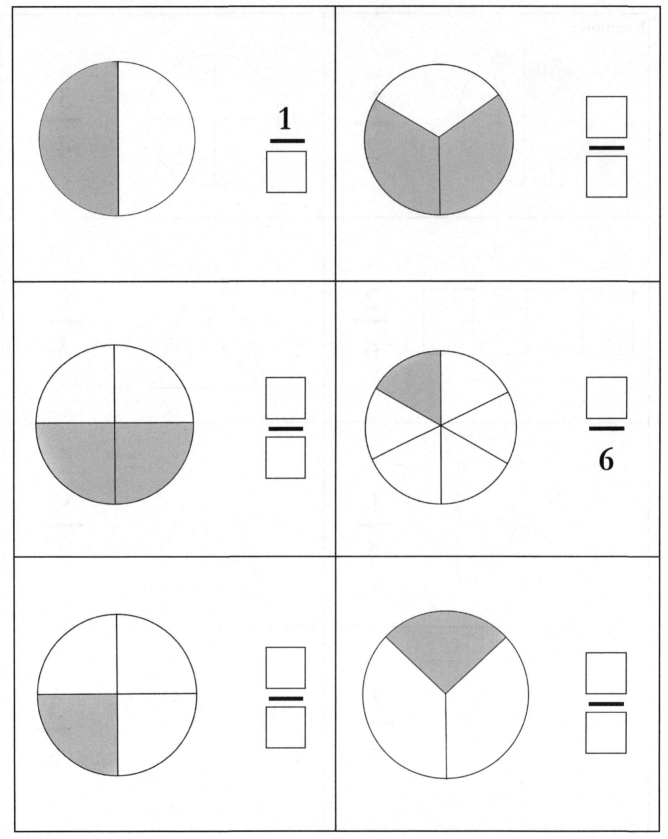

Basic Geometry

Identify and circle the correct 2 D shape:

Example: ⬭	(Circle) / Triangle / Square
1.) △	**Square / Triangle / Circle**
2.) ▢	**Triangle / Circle / Square**
3.) ▭	**Triangle / Square / Rectangle**
4.) ⬠	**Square / Pentagon / Rectangle**
5.) ⬡	**Pentagon / Rectangle / Hexagon**
6.) ⯃	**Pentagon / Octagon / Hexagon**
7.) ▱	**Square / Rectangle / Parallelogram**
8.) ◇	**Rectangle / Diamond / Square**
9.) ⏢	**Rectangle / Square / Trapezoid**

Basic Geometry

Count and write the number of sides (edges) and vertices:

Shape	Name	No. of sides (edges)	No. of vertices
Example:	**Triangle**	**3**	**3**
1.)	**Square**		
2.)	**Rectangle**		
3.)	**Pentagon**		
4.)	**Hexagon**		
5.)	**Octagon**		
6.)	**Parallelogram**		
7.)	**Trapezoid**		

Basic Geometry

Identify and color the geometrical shapes:

Color all the:
- Squares red
- Circles blue
- Triangles green
- Rectangles orange
- Hexagons pink
- Pentagon yellow

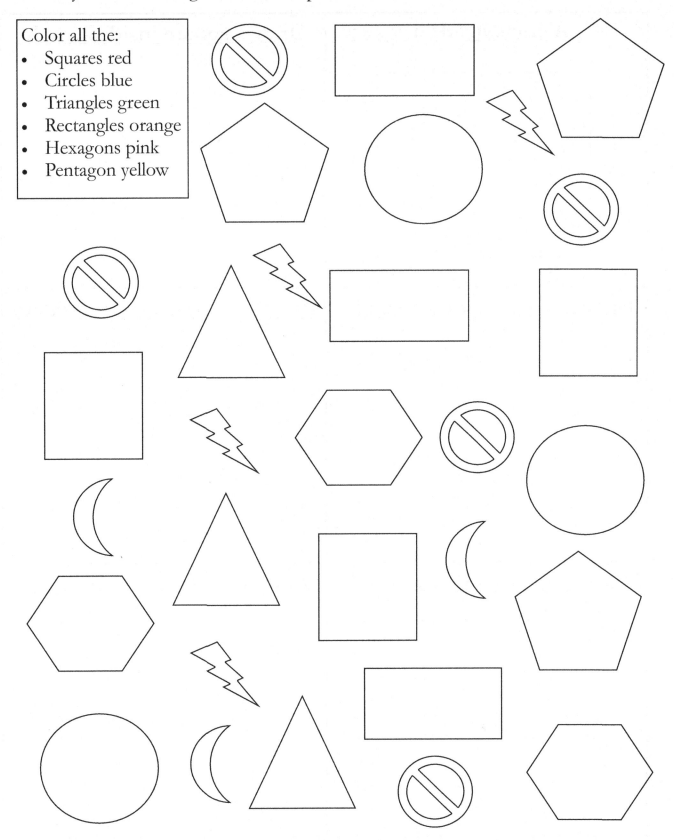

Basic Geometry

Draw the geometrical shapes:

Example: **A circle inside a square.**	**Draw a square inside a circle.**
Draw a circle inside a triangle.	**Draw a triangle inside a square.**
Draw a square inside a rectangle.	**Draw an oval inside a rectangle.**

Basic Geometry

Find the number of triangles in the below shown shapes:

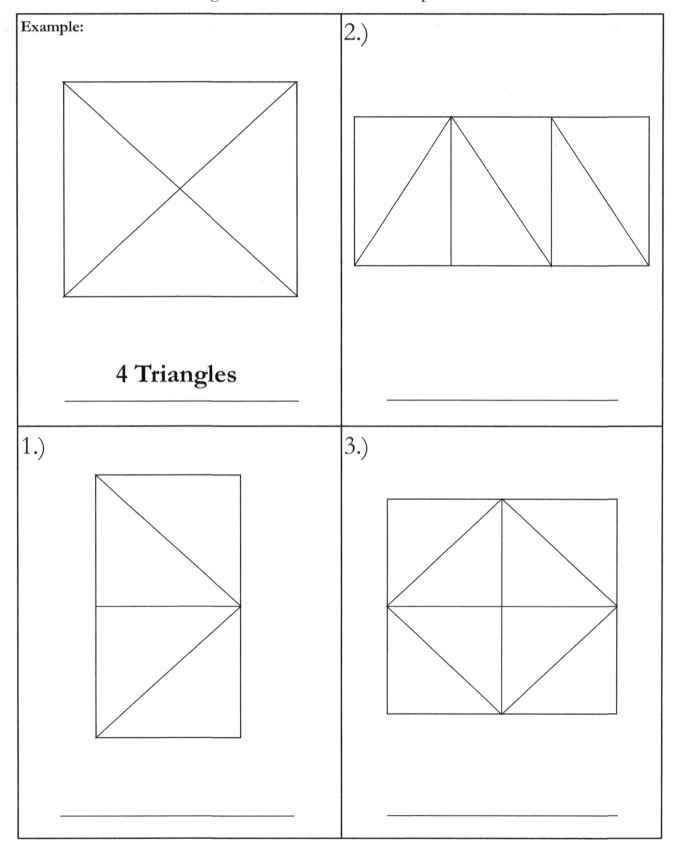

Example:

4 Triangles

2.)

1.)

3.)

Perimeter Of 2D Shapes

Perimeter is the length of the shape's outline. Find the perimeters of the 2D shapes:

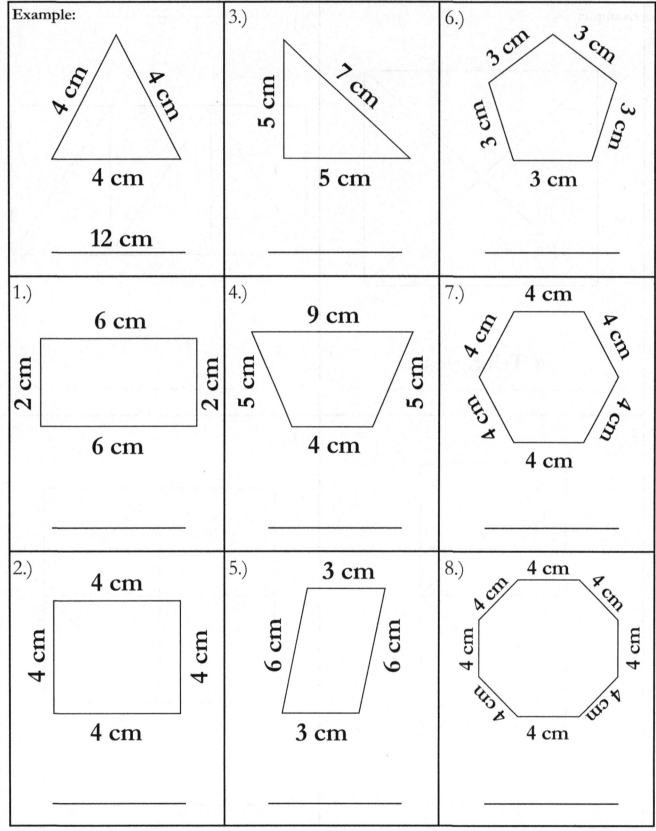

Example:

4 cm   4 cm

4 cm

__12 cm__

3.)

5 cm   7 cm

5 cm

_____

6.)

3 cm   3 cm

3 cm   3 cm

3 cm

_____

1.)

6 cm

2 cm   2 cm

6 cm

_____

4.)

9 cm

5 cm   5 cm

4 cm

_____

7.)

4 cm

4 cm   4 cm

4 cm   4 cm

4 cm

_____

2.)

4 cm

4 cm   4 cm

4 cm

_____

5.)

3 cm

6 cm   6 cm

3 cm

_____

8.)

4 cm

4 cm   4 cm

4 cm   4 cm

4 cm   4 cm

4 cm

_____

Perimeter Of Rectangular Shapes

Find the perimeters of the shapes shown below, if each side of the square is 1 cm:

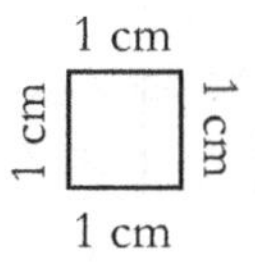

1 cm
1 cm   1 cm
1 cm

Example:	Example:
8 cm	**10 cm**
1.) 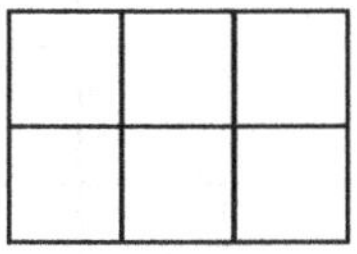	4.) 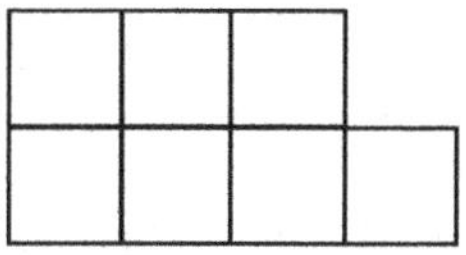
2.) 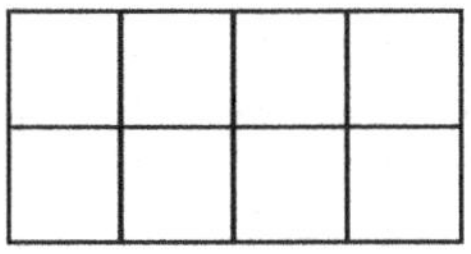	5.) 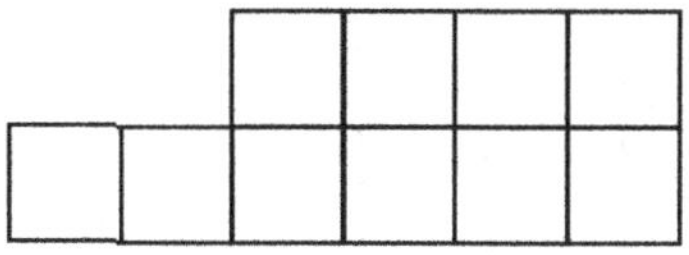
3.) 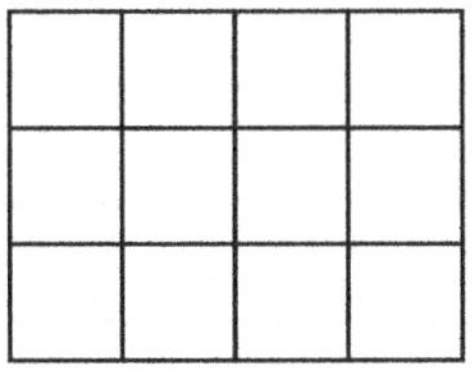	6.) 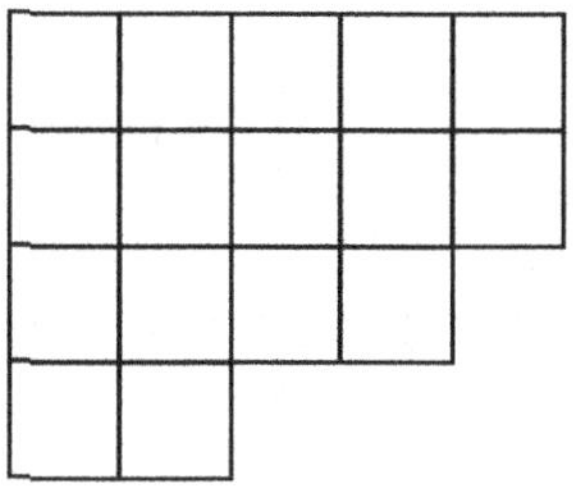

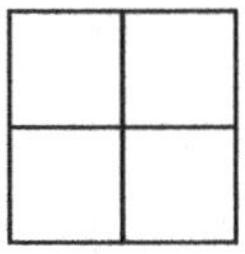

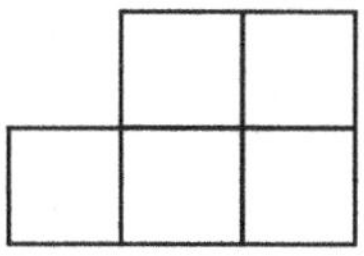

Area Of Rectangular Shapes

Find the area of the shapes shown below, if the area of each square is 1 cm²:

☐ = 1 cm² (square centimeter)

Example:

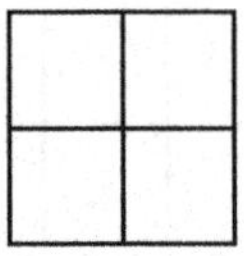

4 cm²
_____

Example:

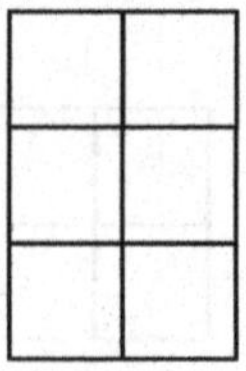

6 cm²
_____

1.)

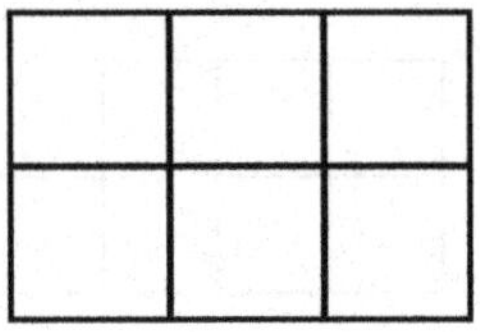

_____

4.)

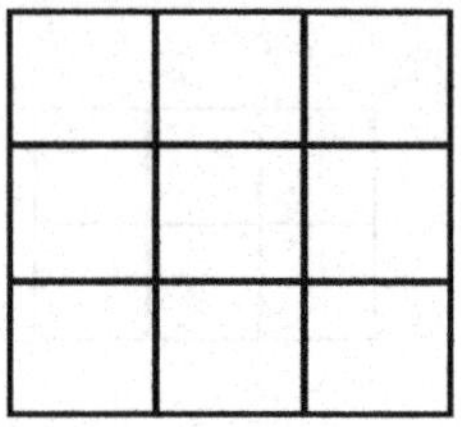

_____

2.)

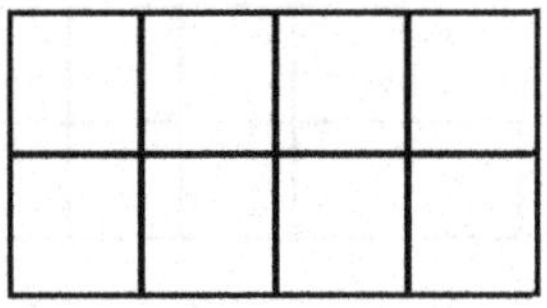

_____

5.)

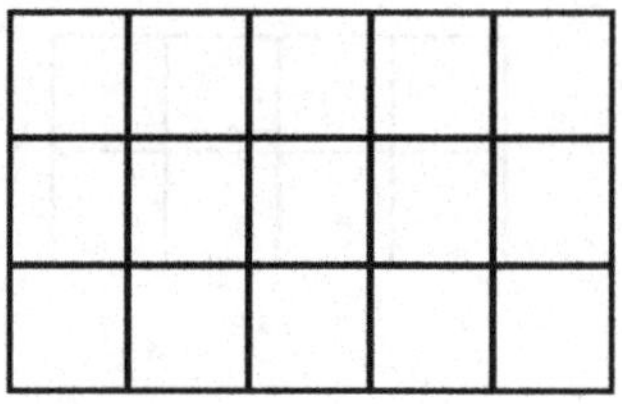

_____

3.)

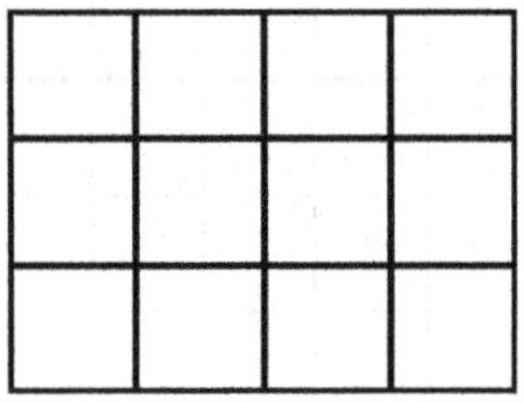

_____

6.)

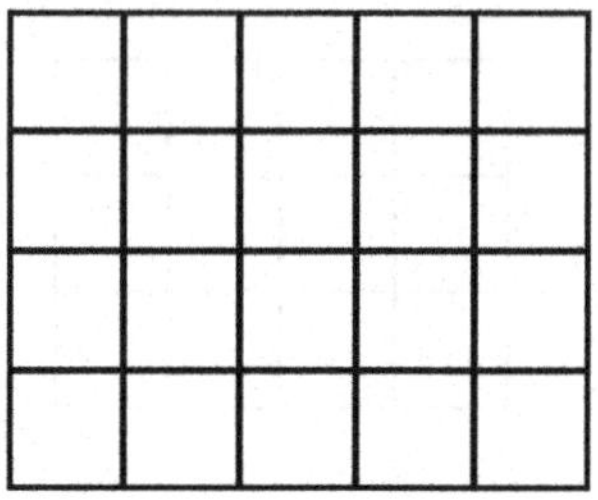

_____

Draw Rectangular Shapes

Draw rectangular shapes according to the given areas below :

Example: Area = 10 square units	Example: Area = 24 square units
Area = 15 square units	**Area = 28 square units**
Area = 20 square units	**Area = 32 square units**

Basic Geometry

Trace the 3-D geometrical shapes:

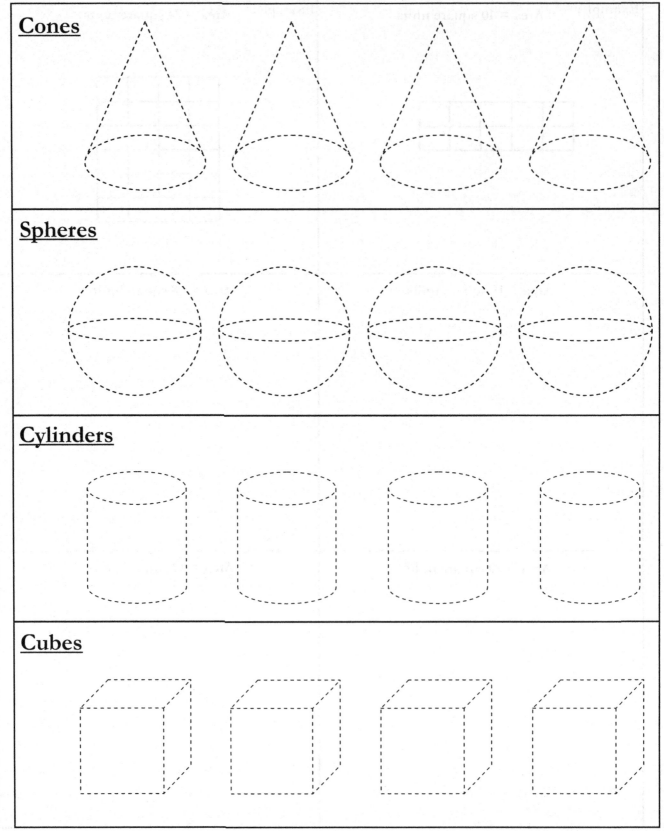

Cones

Spheres

Cylinders

Cubes

Basic Geometry

Circle the 3-D shape that best matches with real world objects:

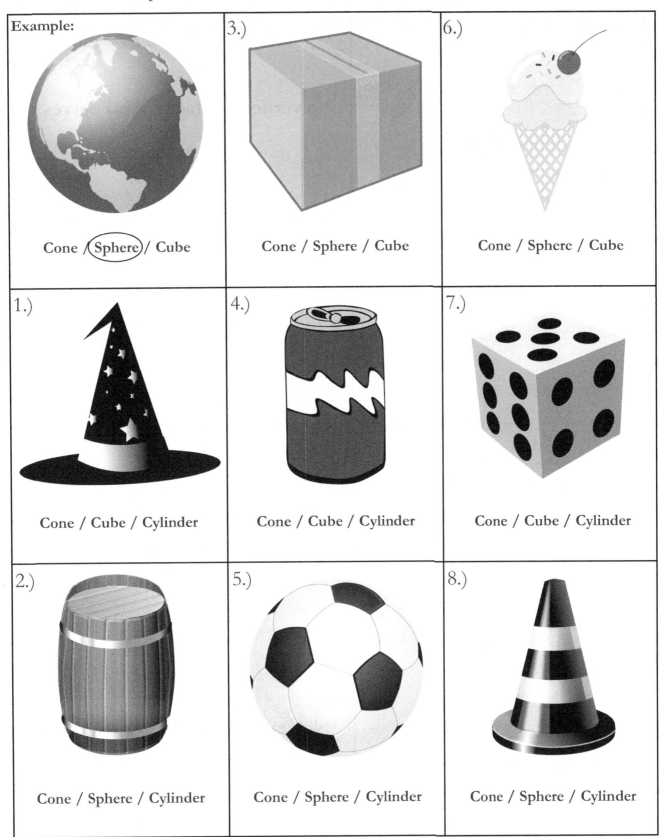

Example:
Cone / (Sphere) / Cube

3.)
Cone / Sphere / Cube

6.)
Cone / Sphere / Cube

1.)
Cone / Cube / Cylinder

4.)
Cone / Cube / Cylinder

7.)
Cone / Cube / Cylinder

2.)
Cone / Sphere / Cylinder

5.)
Cone / Sphere / Cylinder

8.)
Cone / Sphere / Cylinder

Basic Geometry

Draw a line to match the 3-D shape with its correct description:

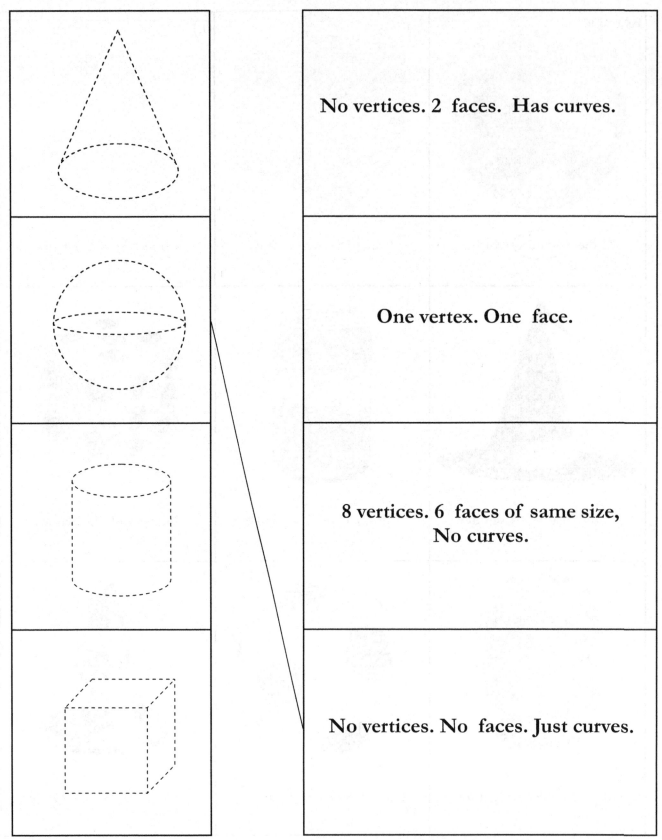

No vertices. 2 faces. Has curves.

One vertex. One face.

8 vertices. 6 faces of same size, No curves.

No vertices. No faces. Just curves.

Basic Measurements

Measure the height using an inch and centimeter scale (round to the nearest figures):

1.) **Pencil**	2.) **Carrot**	3.) **Scarecrow**
_____ inches	_____ inches	_____ inches
_____ centimeters	_____ centimeters	_____ centimeters

Basic Measurements

Measure the height using an inch and centimeter scale (round to the nearest figures):

1.) **Key**	2.) **Shovel**	3.) **Spanner Wrench**
_____ inches	_____ inches	_____ inches
_____ centimeters	_____ centimeters	_____ centimeters

Basic Measurements

Measure the height using an inch and centimeter scale (round to the nearest figures):

1.) **Ostrich**	2.) **Tree**	3.) **Guitar**
_____ inches	_____ inches	_____ inches
_____ centimeters	_____ centimeters	_____ centimeters

Basic Measurements

Write the unit in inches or feet (1 foot = 12 inch):

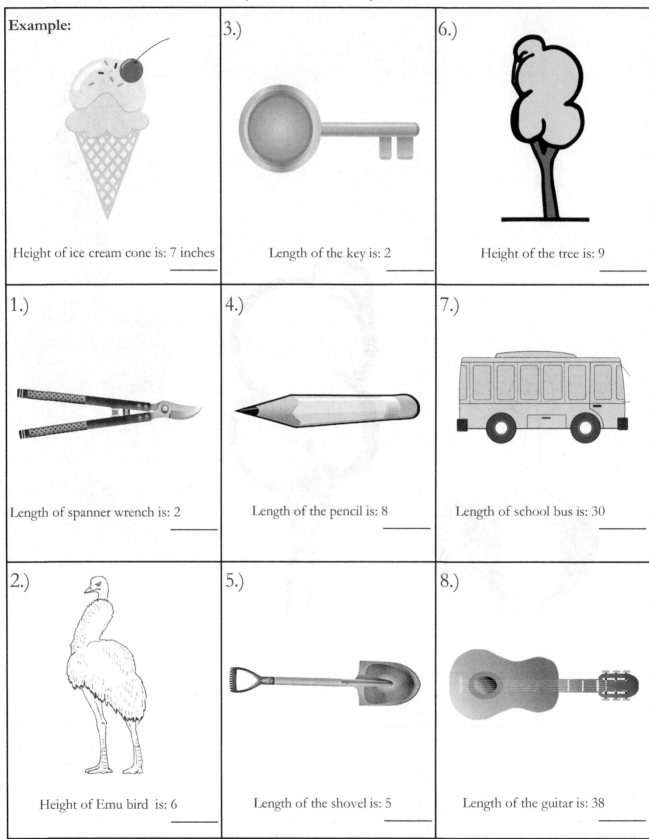

Example:

Height of ice cream cone is: 7 inches _____

3.)

Length of the key is: 2 _____

6.)

Height of the tree is: 9 _____

1.)

Length of spanner wrench is: 2 _____

4.)

Length of the pencil is: 8 _____

7.)

Length of school bus is: 30 _____

2.)

Height of Emu bird is: 6 _____

5.)

Length of the shovel is: 5 _____

8.)

Length of the guitar is: 38 _____

Basic Measurements

Write the unit in meters or centimeters (1 meter = 100 centimeter):

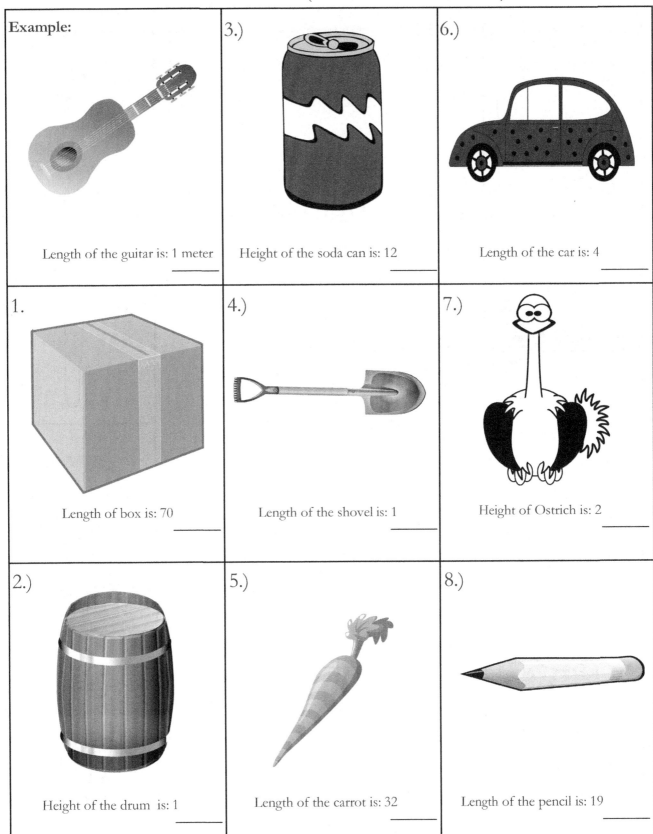

Example:

Length of the guitar is: 1 meter

3.)

Height of the soda can is: 12 _____

6.)

Length of the car is: 4 _____

1.

Length of box is: 70 _____

4.)

Length of the shovel is: 1 _____

7.)

Height of Ostrich is: 2 _____

2.)

Height of the drum is: 1 _____

5.)

Length of the carrot is: 32 _____

8.)

Length of the pencil is: 19 _____

Weight Units (Ounces, Pounds & Tons)

Draw a line to match the objects with the correct weight units:

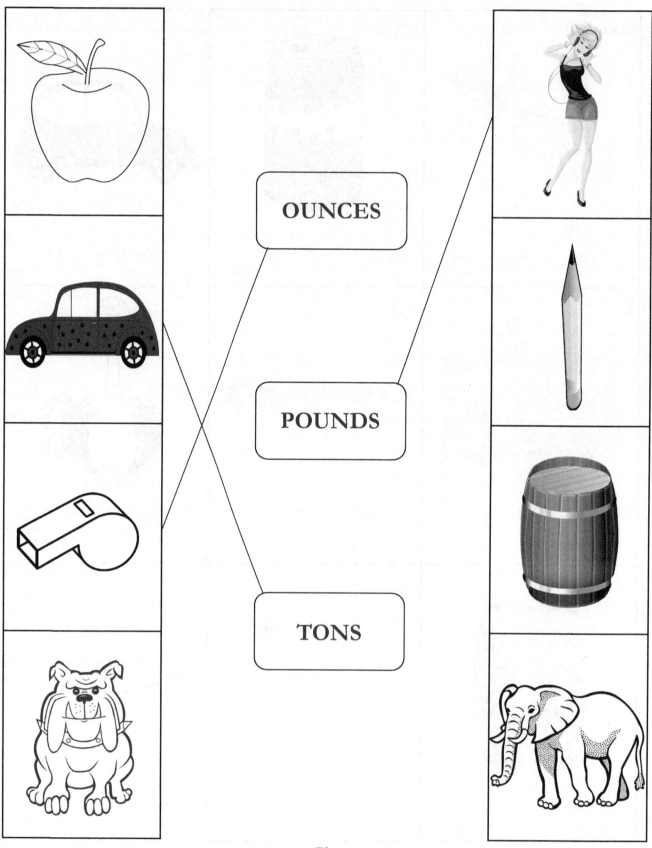

OUNCES

POUNDS

TONS

Weight Units (Grams & Kilograms)

Draw a line to match the objects with the correct weight units:

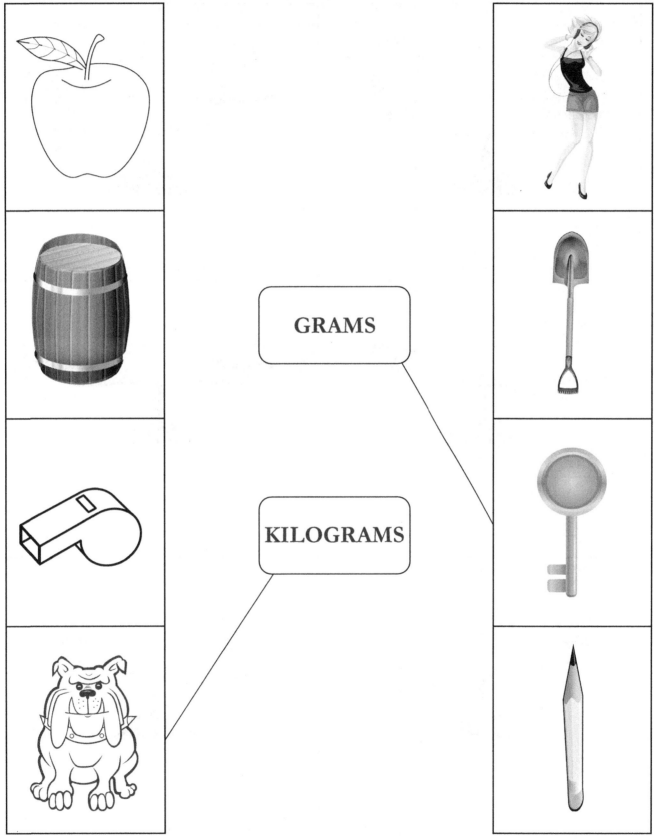

GRAMS

KILOGRAMS

Measure Weights

Fill in the blanks with 'heavier than', 'lighter than', and 'same as':

Example:

The globe weighs the
same as the football.

3.)

The baseball weighs
_____ the basketball.

1.)

The apple weighs
_____ the pencil.

4.)

The guitar weighs the
_____ the shovel.

2.)

The soda can weighs
_____ the books.

5.)

The drum weighs
_____ the dog.

Measure Weights

Measure weights in pounds (lbs):

Example:

The toy car weighs __2 pounds__ .

3.)

The spanner wrench weighs _____ .

1.)

The baseball weighs _____ .

4.)

The toy bus weighs _____ .

2.)

The soda can weighs _____ .

5.)

The books weigh _____ .

Measure Weights

Measure weights in kilogram (kg):

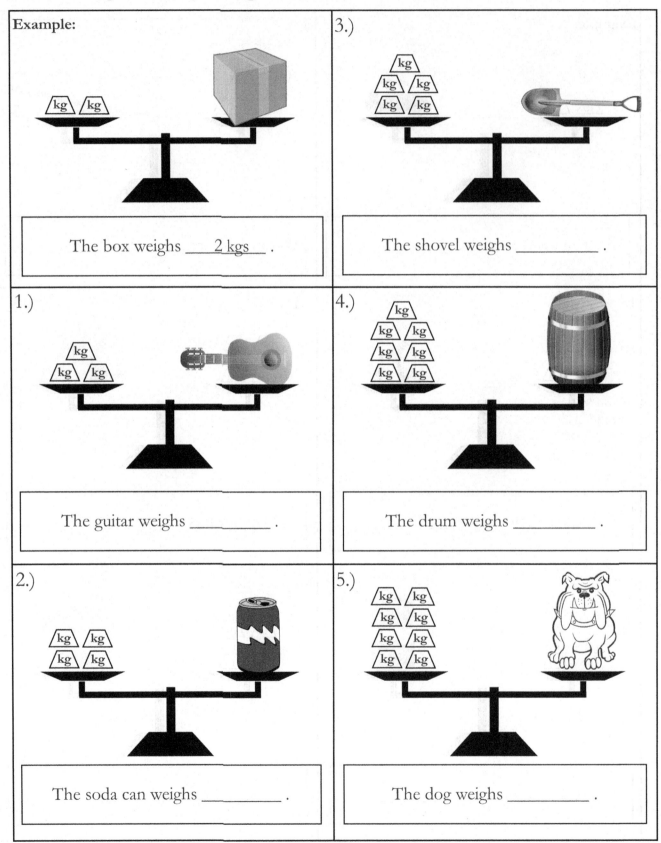

Example:

The box weighs ____2 kgs____ .

3.)

The shovel weighs _____ .

1.)

The guitar weighs _____ .

4.)

The drum weighs _____ .

2.)

The soda can weighs _____ .

5.)

The dog weighs _____ .

Measure Capacity (Gallon)

Find whether the below objects can hold less than or more than 1 gallon (16 cups):

Example: Juice Pack

(Less than) / More than

3.) Aquarium

Less than / More than

6.) Milk Carton

Less than / More than

1.) Teapot

Less than / More than

4.) Soda Can

Less than / More than

7.) Fire Truck

Less than / More than

2.) Coffee Mug

Less than / More than

5.) Bathtub

Less than / More than

8.) Sunscreen Bottle

Less than / More than

Measure Capacity (Liter)

Find whether the below objects can hold less than or more than 1 liter (1000 ml):

Example:

Bathtub

Less than / More than

3.) Yogurt Cup

Less than / More than

6.) Aquarium

Less than / More than

1.) Dropper

Less than / More than

4.) Drum Barrel

Less than / More than

7.) Fire Truck

Less than / More than

2.) Tea Cup

Less than / More than

5.) Sunscreen Bottle

Less than / More than

8.) Juice Pack

Less than / More than

Thermometer Reading (Fahrenheit)

Write the correct temperatures shown in the thermometers below in Fahrenheit:

Example:	2.)	4.)	6.)
10 °F	___ °F	___ °F	___ °F

1.)	3.)	5.)	7.)
___ °F	___ °F	___ °F	___ °F

Thermometer Reading (Celsius)

Write the correct temperatures shown in the thermometers below in Celsius:

Example:	2.)	4.)	6.)
− 10 °C	___ °C	___ °C	___ °C

1.)	3.)	5.)	7.)
___ °C	___ °C	___ °C	___ °C

US Money

Draw a line to match the US currencies with its name:

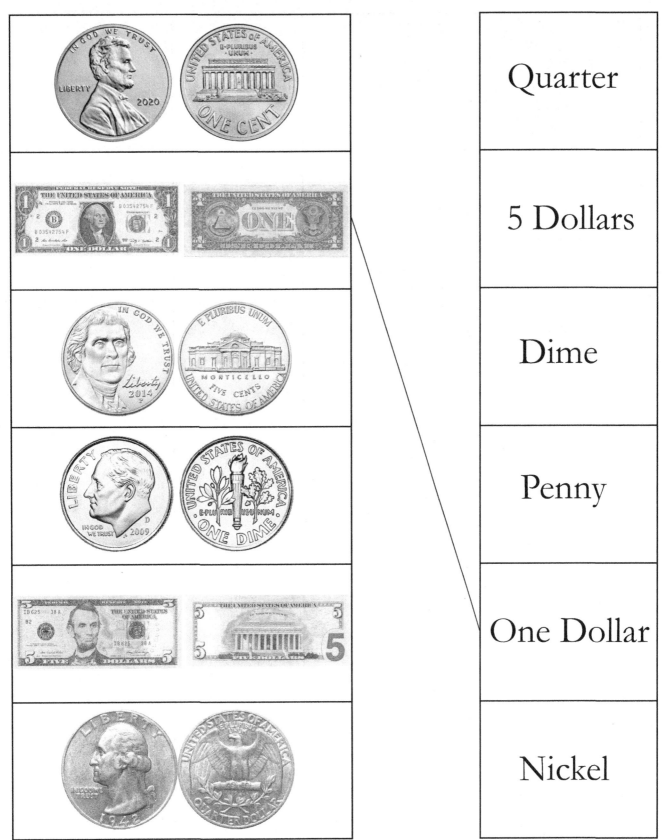

	Quarter
	5 Dollars
	Dime
	Penny
	One Dollar
	Nickel

US Money

Draw a line to match the US currencies with its name:

	25¢
	$5
	10¢
	1¢
	$1
	5¢

US Money

Count the US currencies and write the sum in the box:

Example:	43¢
1.)	
2.)	
3.)	
4.)	
5.)	
6.)	

US Money

Write the US money in words:

Example: $0.75	Zero dollars seventy five cents
$0.81	
$19.78	
$3.56	
$7.48	
$8.93	
$17.11	
$0.35	
$0.99	
$80.62	

US Money

Write the correct amount :

Example: Five dollars seventy six cents	**$5.76**
Zero dollars thirty eight cents	1.)
Nineteen dollars seventy eight cents	2.)
Zero dollars seventeen cents	3.)
Twenty dollars five cents	4.)
Zero dollars forty seven cents	5.)
Sixty five dollars fifty nine cents	6.)
Zero dollars eighty eight cents	7.)
Ninety two dollars ninety three cents	8.)
Zero dollars ninety eight cents	9.)

Canadian Money

Draw a line to match the Canadian coin with its name:

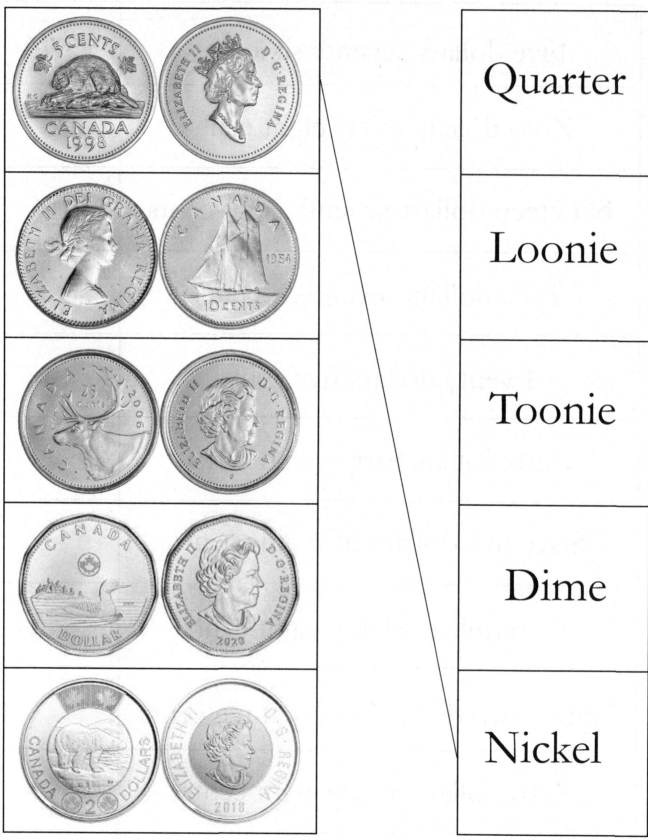

Quarter

Loonie

Toonie

Dime

Nickel

Canadian Money

Draw a line to match the Canadian coin with its value:

	25¢
	$1
	$2
	10¢
	5¢

Canadian Money

Count the Canadian coins and write the sum in the box:

Example:	80¢
1.)	
2.)	
3.)	
4.)	
5.)	
6.)	

Canadian Money

Write the Canadian money in words:

Example: **$6.87**	Six dollars eighty seven cents
$0.98	
$0.35	
$13.79	
$0.60	
$8.88	
$9.96	
$3.58	
$0.69	
$98.87	

Canadian Money

Write the correct amount :

Example: Zero dollars seventy nine cents	**$0.79**
Forty five dollars twenty eight cents	1.)
Four dollars fifty six cents	2.)
Nine dollars forty five cents	3.)
Zero dollars eighty three cents	4.)
Twenty seven dollars forty two cents	5.)
Seven dollars forty five cents	6.)
Zero dollars seventy two cents	7.)
Eight dollars thirty five cents	8.)
Zero dollars sixty eight cents	9.)

UK Money

Draw a line to match the UK coin with its name:

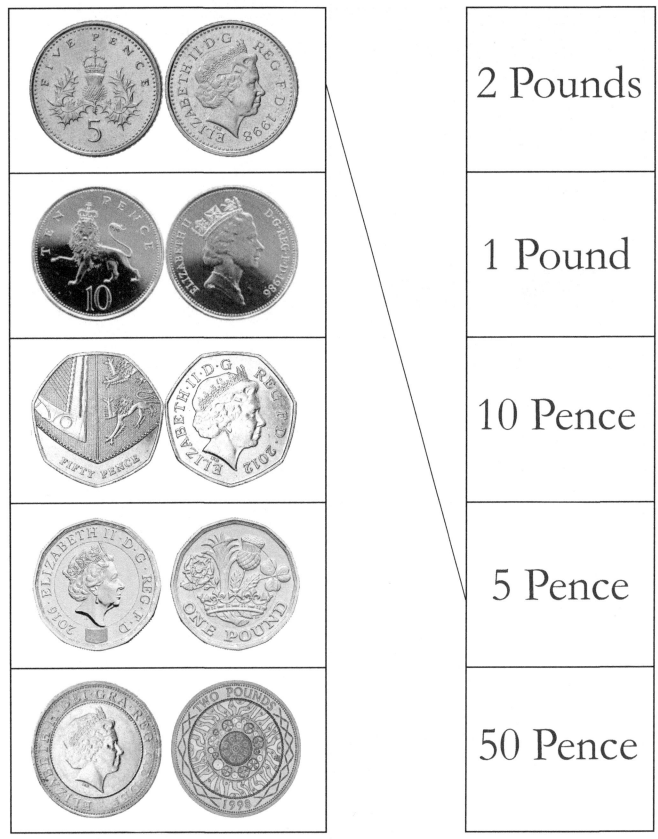

2 Pounds
1 Pound
10 Pence
5 Pence
50 Pence

UK Money

Draw a line to match the UK coin with its value:

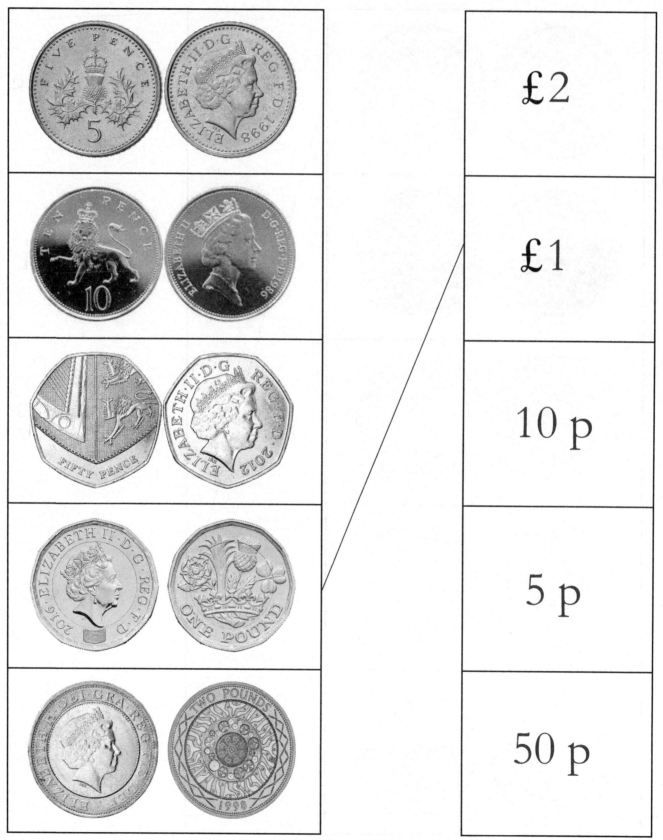

£2

£1

10 p

5 p

50 p

UK Money

Count the UK coins and write the sum in the box:

Example:	**85 p**
1.)	
2.)	
3.)	
4.)	
5.)	
6.)	

UK Money

Write the UK money in words:

Example: £84.78	Eighty four pounds seventy eight pence
£93.30	
£25.43	
£5.36	
£7.18	
£8.32	
£0.93	
£19.88	
£0.68	
£62.36	

UK Money

Write the correct amount :

Example: Eighty seven pence	**£0.87**
Six pounds fifty nine pence	1.)
Sixty four pence	2.)
Forty three pounds fifty eight pence	3.)
Ten pounds ninety two pence	4.)
Two pounds fifty three pence	5.)
Forty eight pounds seventy one pence	6.)
Five pounds forty five cents	7.)
Ninety five pounds seventy eight pence	8.)
Thirteen pounds seventy three pence	9.)

Telling Time

Write the time (in whole hours) below each clock:

Example:

3:00

3.)

6.)

1.)

4.)

7.)

2.)

5.)

8.)

Drawing Time

Draw the time (in whole hours) for each clock below:

Example:

3:00

3.)

6:00

6.)

9:00

1.)

1:00

4.)

5:00

7.)

8:00

2.)

7:00

5.)

11:00

8.)

4:00

Telling Time

Write the time (in half hours) below each clock:

Example:

3:30

1.)

2.)

3.)

4.)

5.)

6.)

7.)

8.)

Drawing Time

Draw the time (in half hours) for each clock below:

Example:

3:30

3.)

5:30

6.)

9:30

1.)

7:30

4.)

12:30

7.)

1:30

2.)

11:30

5.)

10:30

8.)

3:30

Telling Time

Write the time (in quarters) below each clock:

Example: **3:45**

Example: **9:15**

5.)

1.)

3.)

6.)

2.)

4.)

7.)

Drawing Time

Draw the time (in quarters) for each clock below:

Example: 3:45

Example: 9:15

5.) 5:45

1.) 1:45

3.) 2:45

6.) 8:15

2.) 11:45

4.) 10:15

7.) 4:45

Tally Marks

Count each animal or insect, draw tally marks, and write the number:

ANIMAL	TALLY MARKS	NUMBER
Example: 🐱	‖‖‖ ‖‖‖	8
1.) 🐻		
2.) 🐣		
3.) 🐝		

TOTAL

Tally Marks

Count each geometrical shape, draw tally marks for each, and write the number:

SHAPES	TALLY MARKS	NUMBER
1.) ⬭		
2.) △		
3.) ▢		
4.) ▭		

TOTAL

Tally Marks

Count each item, draw tally marks for each, and write the number:

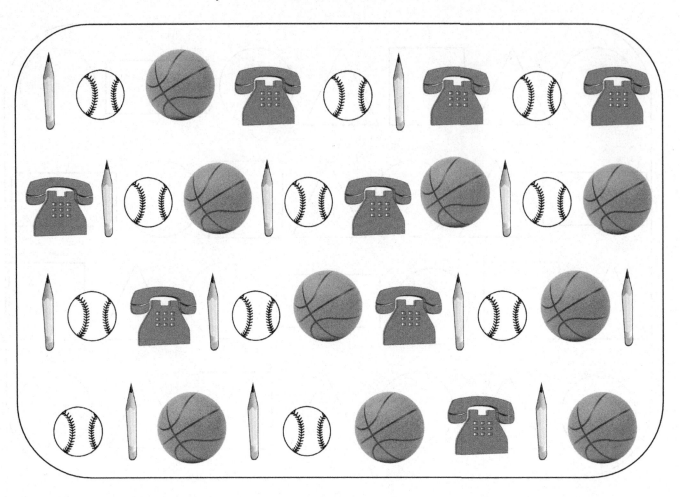

ITEMS	TALLY MARKS	NUMBER
1.)		
2.)		
3.)		
4.)		

TOTAL

110

Answers

Page 5:
1.) 50 2.) 80 3.) 80 4.) 90 5.) 90 6.) 60 7.) 40 8.) 30 9.) 60 10.) 90 11.) 100 12.) 40 13.) 40 14.) 30 15.) 30 16.) 40 17.) 80 18.) 20 19.) 80 20.) 80 21.) 70 22.) 40 23.) 10 24.) 70 25.) 70 26.) 60 27.) 100

Page 6:
1.) 300 2.) 700 3.) 700 4.) 800 5.) 1000 6.) 400 7.) 300 8.) 600 9.) 400 10.) 300 11.) 200 12.) 300 13.) 500 14.) 200 15.) 800 16.) 800 17.) 700 18.) 400 19.) 900 20.) 200 21.) 200 22.) 800 23.) 700 24.) 600 25.) 200 26.) 1000 27.) 900

Page 7:
1.) 770 2.) 900 3.) 300 4.) 790 5.) 570 6.) 500 7.) 590 8.) 710 9.) 400 10.) 600 11.) 590 12.) 800 13.) 990 14.) 130 15.) 690 16.) 400 17.) 600 18.) 160 19.) 870 20.) 700 21.) 660 22.) 860 23.) 400 24.) 800 25.) 970 26.) 600 27.) 480 28.) 910

Page 8:
1.) 85 2.) 78 3.) 86 4.) 56 5.) 57 6.) 49 7.) 59 8.) 77 9.) 58 10.) 48 11.) 95 12.) 64 13.) 71 14.) 97 15.) 59 16.) 78 17.) 76 18.) 59 19.) 99

Page 9:
1.) 98 2.) 28 3.) 79 4.) 55 5.) 87 6.) 86 7.) 45 8.) 89 9.) 74 10.) 98 11.) 59 12.) 76 13.) 73 14.) 55 15.) 88 16.) 28 17.) 97 18.) 24 19.) 64 20.) 87

Page 10:
1.) 87 2.) 99 3.) 89 4.) 57 5.) 59 6.) 76 7.) 70 8.) 99 9.) 88 10.) 44 11.) 69 12.) 88 13.) 77 14.) 77 15.) 68 16.) 77 17.) 88 18.) 44 19.) 99 20.) 99

Page 11:
1.) 112 2.) 123 3.) 64 4.) 144 5.) 111 6.) 133 7.) 116 8.) 128 9.) 113 10.) 120 11.) 111 12.) 133 13.) 110 14.) 120 15.) 120 16.) 111 17.) 137 18.) 113 19.) 115

Page 12:
1.) 120 2.) 142 3.) 110 4.) 121 5.) 120 6.) 120 7.) 120 8.) 175 9.) 152 10.) 111 11.) 143 12.) 123 13.) 111 14.) 111 15.) 112 16.) 111 17.) 151 18.) 132 19.) 84 20.) 126

Page 13:
1.) 111 2.) 153 3.) 121 4.) 145 5.) 150 6.) 111 7.) 116 8.) 112 9.) 140 10.) 150 11.) 116 12.) 193 13.) 110 14.) 120 15.) 115 16.) 124 17.) 111 18.) 133 19.) 130 20.) 150

Page 14:
1.) 130 2.) 114 3.) 170 4.) 165 5.) 106 6.) 168 7.) 182 8.) 106 9.) 151 10.) 135 11.) 150 12.) 84 13.) 142 14.) 184 15.) 225

Page 15:
1.) 90 2.) 182 3.) 241 4.) 111 5.) 167 6.) 129 7.) 150 8.) 81 9.) 170 10.) 102 11.) 252 12.) 145 13.) 180 14.) 180 15.) 151 16.) 157

Page 16:
1.) 81 2.) 114 3.) 188 4.) 259 5.) 217 6.) 112 7.) 171 8.) 76 9.) 91 10.) 151 11.) 154 12.) 88 13.) 141 14.) 70 15.) 202 16.) 195

Page 17:
1.) 250 2.) 209 3.) 191 4.) 134 5.) 178 6.) 160 7.) 180 8.) 217 9.) 189 10.) 235 11.) 284

Page 18:
1.) 169 2.) 246 3.) 157 4.) 243 5.) 263 6.) 174 7.) 171 8.) 279 9.) 224 10.) 139 11.) 298 12.) 199

Page 19:
1.) 171 2.) 285 3.) 162 4.) 305 5.) 174 6.) 144 7.) 319 8.) 255 9.) 208 10.) 220 11.) 271 12.) 190

Page 20:
1.) 878 2.) 989 3.) 969 4.) 959 5.) 999 6.) 428 7.) 689 8.) 774 9.) 658 10.) 695 11.) 669 12.) 698 13.) 475 14.) 879 15.) 256 16.) 887 17.) 696 18.) 477 19.) 978

Page 21:
1.) 858 2.) 775 3.) 889 4.) 989 5.) 499 6.) 697 7.) 977 8.) 639 9.) 655 10.) 997 11.) 779 12.) 976 13.) 799 14.) 896 15.) 814 16.) 578 17.) 968 18.) 596 19.) 735 20.) 717

Page 22:
1.) 647 2.) 489 3.) 865 4.) 947 5.) 589 6.) 953 7.) 898 8.) 719 9.) 929 10.) 809 11.) 499 12.) 979 13.) 759 14.) 872 15.) 446 16.) 808 17.) 865 18.) 975 19.) 647 20.) 848

Page 23:
1.) 1518 2.) 1233 3.) 1140 4.) 1360 5.) 1320 6.) 1614 7.) 1634 8.) 1221 9.) 1560 10.) 1270 11.) 1419 12.) 1096 13.) 1141 14.) 1359 15.) 1126 16.) 1117 17.) 1331 18.) 1504 19.) 1242

Page 24:
1.) 1300 2.) 1140 3.) 1000 4.) 1212 5.) 1314 6.) 1155 7.) 1136 8.) 1099 9.) 1741 10.) 1243 11.) 1420 12.) 1631 13.) 1322 14.) 898 15.) 1113 16.) 1213 17.) 1111 18.) 1132 19.) 1235 20.) 1295

Page 25:
1.) 1142 2.) 1906 3.) 1111 4.) 1803 5.) 1320 6.) 1233 7.) 1311 8.) 1150 9.) 1412 10.) 1611 11.) 1130 12.) 1419 13.) 1123 14.) 1440 15.) 1611 16.) 1421 17.) 1443 18.) 1520 19.) 1132 20.) 1102

Page 26:
1.) 1783 2.) 2504 3.) 1582 4.) 1812 5.) 2045 6.) 1560 7.) 1623 8.) 2072 9.) 1673 10.) 1497 11.) 2343 12.) 948 13.) 2485 14.) 1936 15.) 1047

Page 27:
1.) 2319 2.) 1271 3.) 1259 4.) 1493 5.) 1970 6.) 1696 7.) 1013 8.) 1758 9.) 1427 10.) 1049 11.) 1259 12.) 1941 13.) 1397 14.) 1012 15.) 836 16.) 1657

Page 28:
1.) 1369 2.) 1846 3.) 1504 4.) 1080 5.) 738 6.) 1932 7.) 1714 8.) 1254 9.) 1992 10.) 1409 11.) 1494 12.) 1658 13.) 2377 14.) 1677 15.) 1979 16.) 1822

Page 29:
1.) 4 2.) 77 3.) 1 4.) 23 5.) 22 6.) 45 7.) 24 8.) 72 9.) 4 10.) 13 11.) 24 12.) 42 13.) 20 14.) 30 15.) 5 16.) 82 17.) 45 18.) 34 19.) 50

Page 30:
1.) 34 2.) 61 3.) 11 4.) 11 5.) 30 6.) 61 7.) 42 8.) 63 9.) 62 10.) 43 11.) 51 12.) 52 13.) 45 14.) 33 15.) 31 16.) 9 17.) 13 18.) 6 19.) 4 20.) 43

Page 31:
1.) 3 2.) 53 3.) 4 4.) 73 5.) 44 6.) 83 7.) 13 8.) 40 9.) 10 10.) 32 11.) 21 12.) 31 13.) 9 14.) 41 15.) 61 16.) 21 17.) 13 18.) 77 19.) 24 20.) 60

Page 32:
1.) 28 2.) 56 3.) 14 4.) 77 5.) 48 6.) 55 7.) 15 8.) 29 9.) 29 10.) 46 11.) 19 12.) 9 13.) 18 14.) 9 15.) 2 16.) 9 17.) 19 18.) 18 19.) 9

Page 33:
1.) 29 2.) 24 3.) 9 4.) 46 5.) 19 6.) 49 7.) 15 8.) 19 9.) 8 10.) 13 11.) 9 12.) 8 13.) 49 14.) 59 15.) 4 16.) 19 17.) 17 18.) 8 19.) 26 20.) 17

Page 34:
1.) 8 2.) 9 3.) 28 4.) 9 5.) 39 6.) 19 7.) 17 8.) 26 9.) 28 10.) 19 11.) 18 12.) 15 13.) 34 14.) 7 15.) 18 16.) 35 17.) 58 18.) 8 19.) 37 20.) 58

Page 35:
1.) 104 2.) 220 3.) 41 4.) 102 5.) 363 6.) 18 7.) 452 8.) 310 9.) 504 10.) 47 11.) 31 12.) 801 13.) 113 14.) 401 15.) 141 16.) 140 17.) 66 18.) 493 19.) 24

Page 36:
1.) 600 2.) 621 3.) 28 4.) 412 5.) 406 6.) 601 7.) 101 8.) 126 9.) 402 10.) 104 11.) 221 12.) 224 13.) 408 14.) 264 15.) 43 16.) 130 17.) 201 18.) 110 19.) 113 20.) 102

Page 37:
1.) 20 2.) 121 3.) 21 4.) 201 5.) 415 6.) 203 7.) 122 8.) 32 9.) 356 10.) 11 11.) 122 12.) 322 13.) 245 14.) 334 15.) 253 16.) 204 17.) 351 18.) 177 19.) 311 20.) 440

Page 38:
1.) 215 2.) 90 3.) 405 4.) 617 5.) 106 6.) 367 7.) 118 8.) 118 9.) 613 10.) 302 11.) 419 12.) 107 13.) 155 14.) 129 15.) 112 16.) 216 17.) 558 18.) 309 19.) 506

Page 39:
1.) 89 2.) 349 3.) 348 4.) 504 5.) 638 6.) 147 7.) 479 8.) 229 9.) 138 10.) 236 11.) 407 12.) 317 13.) 439 14.) 106 15.) 106 16.) 119 17.) 96 18.) 449 19.) 466 20.) 475

Page 40:
1.) 104 2.) 236 3.) 739 4.) 516 5.) 517 6.) 807 7.) 192 8.) 108 9.) 154 10.) 633 11.) 178 12.) 319 13.) 408 14.) 307 15.) 106 16.) 308 17.) 174 18.) 208 19.) 198 20.) 428

Page 41:
1.) 1 2.) 2 3.) 3 4.) 4 5.) 5 6.) 6 7.) 7 8.) 8 9.) 9 10.) 10 11.) 2 12.) 4 13.) 6 14.) 8 15.) 10 16.) 12 17.) 14 18.) 16 19.) 18 20.) 20

Page 42:
1.) 3 2.) 6 3.) 9 4.) 12 5.) 15 6.) 18 7.) 21 8.) 24 9.) 27 10.) 30 11.) 4 12.) 8 13.) 12 14.) 16 15.) 20 16.) 24 17.) 28 18.) 32 19.) 36 20.) 40

Page 43:
1.) 5 2.) 10 3.) 15 4.) 20 5.) 25 6.) 30 7.) 35 8.) 40 9.) 45 10.) 50 11.) 6 12.) 12 13.) 18 14.) 24 15.) 30 16.) 36 17.) 42 18.) 48 19.) 54 20.) 60

Page 44:
1.) 7 2.) 14 3.) 21 4.) 28 5.) 35 6.) 42 7.) 49 8.) 56 9.) 63 10.) 70 11.) 8 12.) 16 13.) 24 14.) 32 15.) 40 16.) 48 17.) 56 18.) 64 19.) 72 20.) 80

Page 45:
1.) 9 2.) 18 3.) 27 4.) 36 5.) 45 6.) 54 7.) 63 8.) 72 9.) 81 10.) 90 11.) 10 12.) 20 13.) 30 14.) 40 15.) 50 16.) 60 17.) 70 18.) 80 19.) 90 20.) 100

Page 46:
2.), 4.), 7.), 9.), 11.)

Page 47:
2.), 4.), 5.), 7.), 10.)

Page 48:
1.), 2.), 4.), 7.), 9.), 10.), 12.)

Page 61:
1.) Triangle 2.) Square 3.) Rectangle 4.) Pentagon 5.) Hexagon 6.) Octagon 7.) Parallelogram 8.) Diamond 9.) Trapezoid

Page 62:
1.) edges = 4, vertices = 4
2.) edges = 4, vertices = 4
3.) edges = 5, vertices = 5
4.) edges = 6, vertices = 6
5.) edges = 8, vertices = 8
6.) edges = 4, vertices = 4
7.) edges = 4, vertices = 4

Page 65:
1.) 4 triangles 2.) 6 triangles 3.) 8 triangles

Page 66:
1.) 16 cm 2.) 16 cm 3.) 17 cm 4.) 23 cm 5.) 18 cm 6.) 15 cm 7.) 24 cm 8.) 32 cm

Page 67:
1.) 10 cm 2.) 12 cm 3.) 14 cm 4.) 12 cm 5.) 16 cm 6.) 18 cm

Page 68:
1.) 6 cm² 2.) 8 cm² 3.) 12 cm² 4.) 9 cm² 5.) 15 cm² 6.) 20 cm²

Page 69:

Area = 15 square units   **Area = 28 square units**

Area = 20 square units   **Area = 32 square units**

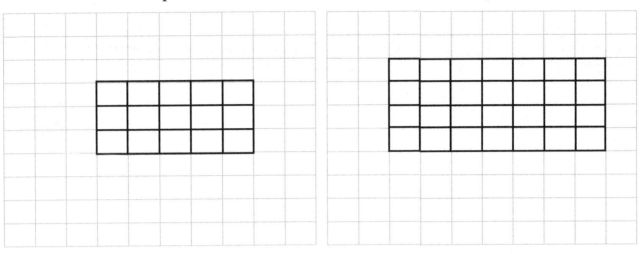

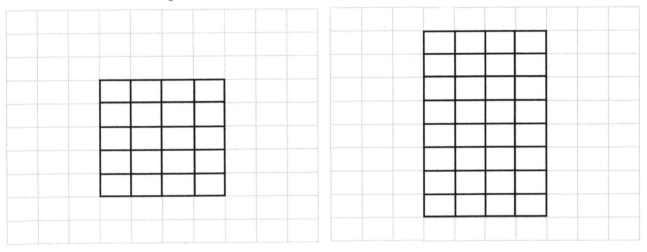

Page 71:
1.) Cone 2.) Cylinder 3.) Cube 4.) Cylinder 5.) Sphere 6.) Cone 7.) Cube 8.) Cone

Page 76:
1.) 2 feet 2.) 6 feet 3.) 2 inches 4.) 8 inches 5.) 5 feet 6.) 9 feet 7.) 30 feet 8.) 38 inches

Page 77:
1.) 70 cm 2.) 1 m 3.) 12 cm 4.) 1 m 5.) 32 cm 6.) 4 m 7.) 2 m 8.) 19 cm

Page 80:
1.) heavier than 2.) lighter than 3.) lighter than 4.) same as 5.) heavier than

Page 81:
1.) 3 pounds (lbs) 2.) 4 pounds (lbs) 3.) 5 pounds (lbs) 4.) 6 pounds (lbs) 5.) 8 pounds (lbs)

Page 82:
1.) 3 kg 2.) 4 kg 3.) 5 kg 4.) 7 kg 5.) 8 kg

Page 83:
1.) less than 2.) less than 3.) more than 4.) less than 5.) more than 6.) less than 7.) more than 8.) less than

Page 84:
1.) less than 2.) less than 3.) less than 4.) more than 5.) less than 6.) more than 7.) more than 8.) less than

Page 85:
1.) 30^0 F 2.) -20^0 F 3.) 0^0 F 4.) -30^0 F 5.) 40^0 F 6.) 20^0 F 7.) -50^0 F

Page 86:
1.) 20^0 C 2.) 30^0 C 3.) -20^0 C 4.) -40^0 C 5.) 10^0 C 6.) 40^0 C 7.) 0^0 C

Page 89:
1.) $1.12 2.) $5.12 3.) 41 ¢ 4.) 95 ¢ 5.) 30 ¢ 6.) $6.15

Page 91:
1.) $0.38 2.) $19.78 3.) $0.17 4.) $20.5 5.) $0.47 6.) $65.59 7.) $0.88 8.) $92.93 9.) $0.98

Page 94:
1.) 50 ¢ 2.) 40 ¢ 3.) 85 ¢ 4.) 55 ¢ 5.) $1.45 6.) $3.35

Page 96:
1.) $45.28 2.) $4.56 3.) $9.45 4.) $0.83 5.) $27.42 6.) $7.45 7.) $0.72 8.) $8.35 9.) $0.68

Page 99:
1.) 45 p 2.) 80 p 3.) 95 p 4.) 90 p 5.) £ 1.75 6.) £ 2.85

Page 101:
1.) £ 6.59 2.) £ 0.64 3.) £ 43.58 4.) £ 10.92 5.) £ 2.53 6.) £ 48.71 7.) £ 5.45 8.) £ 95.78 9.) £ 13.73

Page 102:
1.) 5:00 2.) 11:00 3.) 9:00 4.) 8:00 5.) 4:00 6.) 6:00 7.) 1:00 8.) 7:00

Page 104:
1.) 1:30 2.) 10:30 3.) 9:30 4.) 7:30 5.) 3:30 6.) 5:30 7.) 12:30 8.) 11:30

Page 106:
1.) 2:45 2.) 10:15 3.) 8:15 4.) 4:45 5.) 5:45 6.) 1:45 7.) 11:45

Page 108:

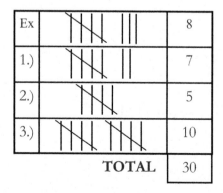

Ex		8
1.)		7
2.)		5
3.)		10
	TOTAL	30

Page 109:

1.)	卌 卌	10
2.)	卌 ||||	9
3.)	卌	5
4.)	||||	4
TOTAL		28

Page 110:

1.)	卌 卌 ||	12
2.)	卌 卌 |	11
3.)	卌 ||||	9
4.)	|||| ||||	8
TOTAL		40

FOR MORE
KIDS ACTIVITY BOOKS
AND
COMPOSITION NOTEBOOKS
BY
ADRISHYA CREATIONS

SCAN ME

Made in the USA
Columbia, SC
08 December 2024

48656760R00065